FARRAR
STRAUS
GIROUX

# BOOKS BY JOHN BERRYMAN

### POETRY

*Poems  (1942)*

*The Dispossessed  (1948)*

*Homage to Mistress Bradstreet  (1956)*

*77 Dream Songs  (1964)*

*Berryman's Sonnets  (1967)*

*Short Poems  (1967)*

*Homage to Mistress Bradstreet*
*and Other Poems  (1968)*

*His Toy, His Dream, His Rest  (1968)*

*The Dream Songs  (1969)*

*Love and Fame  (1970)*

*Delusions, etc.  (1972)*

*Henry's Fate and Other Poems  (1977)*

*The Collected Poems, 1937–1971  (1989)*

### PROSE

*Stephen Crane: A Critical Biography  (1950)*

*The Arts of Reading*
*(with Ralph Ross and Allen Tate)*
*(Crowell)  (1960)*

*Recovery  (1973)*

*The Freedom of the Poet  (1976)*

# THE DREAM SONGS

*John Berryman*

# THE DREAM SONGS

Farrar, Straus and Giroux
New York

Farrar, Straus and Giroux
19 Union Square West, New York 10003

Copyright © 1959, 1962, 1963, 1964, 1965, 1966, 1967, 1968, 1969
by John Berryman
Copyright renewed © 1997 by Kate Donahue
Introduction copyright © 2007 by W. S. Merwin
All rights reserved
Distributed in Canada by Douglas & McIntyre Ltd.
Printed in the United States of America
Originally published in 1969 by Farrar, Straus and Giroux
This paperback edition, 2007

Grateful acknowledgment is made for permission to reprint lines from "The Bridge,"
from *Complete Poems of Hart Crane* by Hart Crane, edited by Marc Simon. Copyright
1933, 1958, 1966 by Liveright Publishing Corporation. Copyright © 1986 by Marc
Simon. Used by permission of Liveright Publishing Corporation.

Library of Congress Control Number: 2006938228
Paperback ISBN-13: 978-0-374-53066-2
Paperback ISBN-10: 0-374-53066-1

Designed by Guy Fleming

www.fsgbooks.com

10  9  8  7  6  5  4  3  2

# Contents

# III

# IV

# VII

xvi

# Author's Note

THIS VOLUME COMBINES 77 *Dream Songs* and *His Toy, His Dream, His Rest*, comprising Books I through VII of a poem whose working title, since 1955, has been *The Dream Songs*.

My most deep thanks are due to the Ingram Merrill Foundation and the John Simon Guggenheim Memorial Foundation for generous help without which the poem would probably never have been finished, at least in its present form. My thanks are due also to the President and the Regents of the University of Minnesota, which awarded me a sabbatical leave at a critical moment in the composition. Acknowledgment is here made also to various editors who printed some of the Songs, especially to Mr Crook and Mr Hamilton of *The Times Literary Supplement*, which printed many early Songs and most of Book IV. British hospitality to foreign poetry, particularly American, makes a bright spot in a sickening century. The editors of the following journals have also been hospitable to some of the Songs: *The Atlantic, Audience, Encounter, Harper's, The Kenyon Review, Minnesota Review, Mundus Artium, New American Review, The New Republic, The New York Review of Books, The Noble Savage, The Observer, Partisan Review, Poetry, Poetry Northwest, Ramparts, Tri-Quarterly, The Virginia Quarterly*, and *The Yale Review*.

The second Song is dedicated to the memory of Daddy Rice who sang and jumped 'Jim Crow' in Louisville in 1828 (London, 1836 and later), and others to friends: Robert Giroux (*7, 364*), John Crowe Ransom (*11*), Howard Munford (*24*), Ralph Ross (*27*), Robert Fitzgerald (*34*), Daniel Hughes (*35*), William Meredith (*36*), the Theodore Morrisons and the Chisholm Gentrys (*37, 38, 39*), Dr A. Boyd Thomes (*54*), Edmund and Elena Wilson (*58*), George

Amberg (*63*), Mark Van Doren (*66*), Allen and Isabella Tate (*70*), Saul Bellow (*75*), Ellen Siegelman (*92*), Philip Siegelman (*180-1*), Dr A. Boyd Thomes (*184*), Maris Thomes (*239, 295*), Robert Lowell (*287*), Adrienne Rich (*294, 307, 362*), Valerie Trueblood (*286, 315*), William Meredith (*320*), Howard Nemerov (*335*), Victoria Bay (*344*).

Many opinions and errors in the Songs are to be referred not to the character Henry, still less to the author, but to the title of the work. It is idle to reply to critics, but some of the people who addressed themselves to the 77 *Dream Songs* went so desperately astray (one apologized about it in print, but who ever sees apologies?) that I permit myself one word. The poem then, whatever its wide cast of characters, is essentially about an imaginary character (not the poet, not me) named Henry, a white American in early middle age sometimes in blackface, who has suffered an irreversible loss and talks about himself sometimes in the first person, sometimes in the third, sometimes even in the second; he has a friend, never named, who addresses him as Mr Bones and variants thereof. Requiescant in pace.

J.B.

# Introduction

## by W. S. Merwin

In 1964, when 77 *Dream Songs* was first published, even readers of
John Berryman's poetry who had followed it from the poems in *The
Dispossessed* (1948) through the poignant dramatic power of *Homage
to Mistress Bradstreet* (1956) and the wrung, resonant dissonances of
*His Thoughts Made Pockets and the Plane Buckt* (1958) were startled by
the impact of this unprecedented book. Separate poems had
appeared here and there in literary reviews, but they could not have
prepared anyone for the cumulative effect of this collection, which
had suddenly arrived like a force of nature, unique and new.

Such astonishment was certainly something that John had wanted.
He had dreamed of it and struggled toward it for what must have
seemed to him an unconscionably long time. The hunger for it was a
craving that had presided over the whole of his youth. He was fifty
in the year that 77 *Dream Songs* was published, and his feelings about
age were influenced by his belonging to a generation of poets who
had grown up in the shadow of T. S. Eliot—or felt they had—and,
partly as a result of that, had felt old before their time. Already in his
thirties, John had seemed much older than, in fact, he was, as though
youth (but not its recurrent anguish and wildness) was far behind
him, absorbed and consumed in study and in the very intensity of his
aspiration. He had always read in the way that he did most things,
with a heated passion, and his memory for poetry and for details of
the lives of poets was compendious and clear. It all seemed to be
present and immediate to him, and endowed with a final authority.
Once, in his thirties, after a bookstore reading of poems by other

poets whom he loved—in this case, Hardy and Yeats—someone had
been so foolish as to ask him whether he did not, perhaps, take these
things too seriously, and he had answered, "They're a matter of life
and death."

His ambition matched his brilliance. It was propelled by psychic
jets that those who knew him made whatever sense of they could.
For years, through the forties and into the fifties, he was bound to
keep comparing his own unimpressive reputation with that of his
friend Robert Lowell, three years his junior, whose second book,
*Lord Weary's Castle*, leaped into national prominence in 1947,
winning the Pulitzer Prize and prompting an essay with a large,
striking photograph in *Life* magazine. Berryman surely knew that
Lowell was constantly playing a private game of ranking
contemporary poets according to varying assessments of his own,
and though public status itself was not a determining factor in his
tabulations, it was something that Lowell observed with a keen
interest, and—it is scarcely surprising—took to be his due. It was not
until 1956, and the acclaim that followed the publication of *Homage
to Mistress Bradstreet*, that Berryman's originality and the importance
of his gifts were accorded the recognition he knew he deserved. He
was not yet forty then, and he was placed at last among other poets
of his remarkable generation who—besides Lowell—were already
known to readers of contemporary poetry: Theodore Roethke,
Delmore Schwartz, Randall Jarrell, Elizabeth Bishop.

It would be eleven more years before 77 *Dream Songs* was
published, and they were years of continuing turmoil and
transformation in his life, his amours, and his academic situation.
The turmoil, some of the transformations it engendered, and some
of the imagery arising from Berryman's vast consumption of alcohol
were alchemized into his poems, coming to represent the agon he

had carried with him from his childhood, an accompaniment as untouchable as a spark and as continuous as an electric current. The torque and intensity of his days were refracted not only in the *Dream Songs* as they began to emerge but in the language he evolved for them. It was a medium as distinctly his own as that of *Finnegans Wake* was finally the language of Joyce.

He would extend the *Dream Songs'* range of subjects after the first ones, but he would not move away from their mode. It would provide the format and the echoes that he would return to in his poetry with recurring, though inconstant, powers, for the rest of his life.

Even in the 77 poems of the first collection of *Dream Songs* the essential attributes of their idiom were fully formed. The originality of their language is flaunted, saved from affectation by the sheer authority and authenticity of the voice it embodies. The verse proceeds with an oddity skating on the edge of comprehensibility and frequently slipping well beyond it. Syntax, tone, diction, and movement—subjects that Berryman pondered fixedly for years— were deliberately arranged, syllable by syllable, cadenzas on carefully tuned strings. But the high artifice was countered by wild liberties taken with grammar, allusion, meter, and every pattern of expectation that the verse suggested. The effect divided—and probably still divides—readers and critics, some finding it inexcusably exasperating, while for others its revelations continue to be primal manifestations of poetry itself.

Other distinguishing traits of the mode became apparent as the songs continued. Berryman's poems had never offered ease of access. His elaborately rearranged word order and sentence structure played with the pitch and current of the verse, taking the reader's attention utterly for granted. John was writing at a time when such an assumption was not uncommon. Since the advent of modernism and the canonization of *The Waste Land*, poetry was commonly expected to be difficult or "obscure." Writings, in prose and verse, that seemed especially pertinent at the time were formally dense, artful, and monumental. Joyce was a dominant exemplar, especially the Joyce of *Ulysses* and *Finnegans Wake*. So were the later poems of Yeats. And Berryman admired Hart Crane, and quoted, with a vividness that was indelible, a quatrain from *The Bridge*:

> Out of some subway scuttle, cell or loft
> A bedlamite speeds to thy parapets,
> Tilting there momently, shrill shirt ballooning,
> A jest falls from the speechless caravan.

In prose, except for Faulkner, most of the guiding presences were European: Kafka, Mann, and Hermann Broch. Among Berryman's contemporaries he was closely aware of Delmore Schwartz and Randall Jarrell, and, despite specific reservations, he had, as a matter of course, a deep admiration for Dylan Thomas. The elder who remained one of his close abiding influences was Gerard Manley Hopkins. For none of these writers was the reader's ease of comprehension a besetting consideration.

John knew many of Hopkins's poems by heart, and would quote phrases and passages, emphasizing the word order and the way accented syllables had been set in the verse like notations in music. He was using lines of Hopkins as touchstones long before he had conceived of the *Dream Songs*.

The *Dream Songs* present with full assurance something else that Berryman had been moving toward for three decades. The poems are not lyrics, in the sense of being articulations of a more or less fictionalized first person. They are narrative and dramatic accounts, and they speak with and through a variety of voices that are sometimes not clearly identified even when they are named. There is the ever-present Henry in a foreground that shifts like a series of projections on a stage, or the world seen through inebriation or, as the title suggests, in dreams. And there is the responsive, echoing figure—part chorus, part wise fool—a persistent counterpart who speaks in stilted old-time minstrel blackface. Beginning with the second dream song, this figure and what may be other voices address Henry (or so it seems) as "Mr. Bones" or "Sir Bones," but in some exchanges it is uncertain who is addressing whom. The dialogue continues like the script of a disjointed film throughout the series.

Charles Thornbury, in his introduction to Berryman's *Collected Poems 1937–1971* (which does not include the *Dream Songs*), writes of Berryman's search for a way of articulating his own personality, or aspects of it, in his poems, in the era of the New Criticism and of Eliot's prevalent dictum of "the impersonality of the poet." Thornbury quotes from Berryman's revealing letters to his mother (published as *We Dream of Honour* by W. W. Norton in 1988), passages that tell of his coming to think of the voices in his poems, including those that might seem to represent the author, as voices of characters in drama. The different personae, in turn, shift their shapes, their presences, their identities insofar as they have any such thing, sometimes in midsentence, with the mere changing of the indicative pronoun. The reader's resulting uncertainty is just what Berryman intended. A reader was meant to keep wondering who is talking to whom. Berryman believed that the hallucinatory effect of such doubt and ambiguity added to the richness of the passages that produced it.

Often it did, and still does. And a presumption of the artifice he had developed was that a reading of these poems would not happen once and for all but would be repeated until the poems became part of a familiar continuity, not finished but surviving. This unreasonable faith may in fact be one of the underlying conditions of poetry. It is confirmed occasionally in the ordinary world by writing whose originality transcends all formulas, and outlasts the conventions and expectations of its time. Such an achievement may happen—as John Berryman pointed out in the writing of others—in only a few miraculous lines out of a whole life's work. Or it may, with major talents, include the lifework as a whole, with its great radiant moments and its lapses as well, because of their relation to a singular voice and vision. Berryman's poetry, I believe, is among the major achievements of his gifted and bedeviled generation, and the *Dream Songs*—intimate, elusive, wild, unbearable, beautiful—are its summation.

W. S. MERWIN was born in New York City in 1927. From 1949 to 1951 he worked as a tutor in France, Majorca, and Portugal; for several years after that he made the greater part of his living by translating from French, Spanish, Latin, and Portuguese. His many awards include the 2005 National Book Award for Poetry for *Migration: New and Selected Poems* (2005), the Pulitzer Prize in Poetry, the Tanning Prize for Poetry, the Bollingen Prize for Poetry, the Lannan Lifetime Literary Achievement Award, and the Ruth Lily Poetry Prize, as well as fellowships from the Rockefeller and Guggenheim foundations and the National Endowment for the Arts. He is the author of dozens of books of poetry and prose; his most recent volume of poems is *Present Company* (2005). For the past thirty years he has lived in Hawaii.

# 77 DREAM SONGS

*To Kate, and to Saul*

'THOU DREWEST NEAR IN THE DAY'

# I

Huffy Henry hid     the day,
unappeasable Henry sulked.
I see his point,—a trying to put things over.
It was the thought that they thought
they could *do* it made Henry wicked & away.
But he should have come out and talked.

All the world like a woolen lover
once did seem on Henry's side.
Then came a departure.
Thereafter nothing fell out as it might or ought.
I don't see how Henry, pried
open for all the world to see, survived.

What he has now to say is a long
wonder the world can bear & be.
Once in a sycamore I was glad
all at the top, and I sang.
Hard on the land wears the strong sea
and empty grows every bed.

# Big Buttons, Cornets: the advance

The jane is zoned! no nightspot here, no bar
there, no sweet freeway, and no premises
for business purposes,
no loiterers or needers. Henry are
baffled. Have ev'ybody head for Maine,
utility-man take a train?

Arrive a time when all coons lose dere grip,
but is he come? Le's do a hoedown, gal,
one blue, one shuffle,
if them is all you seem to réquire. Strip,
ol banger, skip us we, sugar; so hang on
one chaste evenin.

—Sir Bones, or Galahad: astonishin
yo legal & yo good. Is you feel well?
Honey dusk do sprawl.
—Hit's hard. Kinged or thinged, though, fling & wing.
Poll-cats are coming, hurrah, hurray.
I votes in my hole.

# A Stimulant for an Old Beast

Acacia, burnt myrrh, velvet, pricky stings.
—I'm not so young but not so very old,
said screwed-up lovely 23.
A final sense of being right out in the cold,
unkissed.
(—My psychiatrist can lick your psychiatrist.) Women get under
   things.

All these old criminals sooner or later
have had it. I've been reading old journals.
Gottwald & Co., out of business now.
Thick chests quit. Double agent, Joe.
She holds her breath like a seal
and is whiter & smoother.

Rilke was a *jerk.*
I admit his griefs & music
& titled spelled all-disappointed ladies.
A threshold worse than the circles
where the vile settle & lurk,
Rilke's. As I said,—

# 4

Filling her compact & delicious body
with chicken páprika, she glanced at me
twice.
Fainting with interest, I hungered back
and only the fact of her husband & four other people
kept me from springing on her

or falling at her little feet and crying
'You are the hottest one for years of night
Henry's dazed eyes
have enjoyed, Brilliance.' I advanced upon
(despairing) my spumoni. —Sir Bones: is stuffed,
de world, wif feeding girls.

—Black hair, complexion Latin, jewelled eyes
downcast . . . The slob beside her      feasts . . . What wonders is
she sitting on, over there?
The restaurant buzzes. She might as well be on Mars.
Where did it all go wrong? There ought to be a law against Henry.
—Mr. Bones: there is.

Henry sats in de bar & was odd,
off in the glass from the glass,
at odds wif de world & its god,
his wife is a complete nothing,
St Stephen
getting even.

Henry sats in de plane & was gay.
Careful Henry nothing said aloud
but where a Virgin out of cloud
to her Mountain dropt in light,
his thought made pockets & the plane buckt.
'Parm me, lady.' 'Orright.'

Henry lay in de netting, wild,
while the brainfever bird did scales;
Mr Heartbreak, the New Man,
come to farm a crazy land;
an image of the dead on the fingernail
of a newborn child.

# 6

## *A Capital at Wells*

During the father's walking—how he look
down by now in soft boards, Henry, pass
and what he feel or no, who know?—
as during hís broad father's, all the breaks
& ill-lucks of a thriving pioneer
back to the flying boy in mountain air,

Vermont's child to go out, and while Keats sweat'
for hopeless inextricable lust, Henry's fate,
and Ethan Allen was a calling man,
all through the blind one's dream of the start,
when Day was killing Porter and had to part
lovers for ever, fancy if you can,

while the cardinals' guile to keep Aeneas out
was failing, while in some hearts Chinese doubt
inscrutably was growing, toward its end,
and a starved lion by a water-hole
clouded with gall, while Abelard was whole,
these grapes of stone were being proffered, friend.

8

# 'The Prisoner of Shark Island'
# with Paul Muni

Henry is old, old; for Henry remembers
Mr Deeds' tuba, & the Cameo,
& the race in *Ben Hur*,—*The Lost World*, with sound,
& *The Man from Blankley's*, which he did not dig,
nor did he understand one caption of,
bewildered Henry, while the Big Ones laughed.

Now Henry is unmistakably a Big One.
Fúnnee; he don't féel so.
He just stuck around.
The German & the Russian films into
Italian & Japanese films turned, while many
were prevented from making it.

He wishing he could squirm again where Hoot
is just ahead of rustlers, where William S
forgoes some deep advantage, & moves on,
where Hashknife Hartley having the matter taped
the rats are flying. For the rats
have moved in, mostly, and this is for real.

The weather was fine. They took away his teeth,
white & helpful; bothered his backhand;
halved his green hair.
They blew out his loves, his interests. 'Underneath,'
(they called in iron voices) 'understand,
is nothing. So there.'

The weather was very fine. They lifted off
his covers till he showed, and cringed & pled
to see himself less.
They installed mirrors till he flowed. 'Enough'
(murmured they) 'if you will watch Us instead,
yet you may saved be. Yes.'

The weather fleured. They weakened all his eyes,
and burning thumbs into his ears, and shook
his hand like a notch.
They flung long silent speeches. (Off the hook!)
They sandpapered his plumpest hope. (So capsize.)
They took away his crotch.

Deprived of his enemy, shrugged to a standstill
horrible Henry, foaming. Fan their way
toward him who will
in the high wood: the officers, their rest,
with p. a. echoing: his girl comes, say,
conned in to test

if he's still human, see: she love him, see,
therefore she get on the Sheriff's mike & howl
'Come down, come down'.
Therefore he un-budge, furious. He'd flee
but only Heaven hangs over him foul.
At the crossways, downtown,

he dreams the folks are buying parsnips & suds
and paying rent to foes. He slipt & fell.
It's golden here in the snow.
A mild crack: a far rifle. Bogart's duds
truck back to Wardrobe. Fancy the brain from hell
held out so long. Let go.

There were strange gatherings. A vote would come
that would be no vote. There would come a rope.
Yes. There would come a rope.
Men have their hats down. "Dancing in the Dark"
will see him up, car-radio-wise. So many, some
won't find a rut to park.

It is in the administration of rhetoric,
on these occasions, that—not the fathomless heart—
the thinky death consists;
his chest is pinched. The enemy are sick,
and so is us of. Often, to rising trysts,
like this one, drove he out

and the gasps of love, after all, had got him ready.
However things hurt, men hurt worse. He's stark
to be jerked onward?
Yes. In the headlights he got' keep him steady,
leak not, look out over. This' hard work,
boss, wait' for The Word.

His mother goes. The mother comes & goes.
Chen Lung's too came, came and crampt & then
that dragoner's mother was gone.
It seem we don't have no good bed to lie on,
forever. While he drawing his first breath,
while skinning his knees,

while he was so beastly with love for Charlotte Coquet
he skated up & down in front of her house
wishing he could, sir, die,
while being bullied & he dreamt he could fly—
during irregular verbs—them world-sought bodies
safe in the Arctic lay:

Strindberg rocked in his niche, the great Andrée
by muscled Fraenkel under what's of the tent,
torn like then limbs, by bears
over fierce decades, harmless. Up in pairs
go we not, but we have a good bed.
I have said what I had to say.

# 12

## *Sabbath*

There is an eye, there was a slit.
Nights walk, and confer on him fear.
The strangler tree, the dancing mouse
confound his vision; then they loosen it.
Henry widens. How did Henry House
himself ever come here?

Nights run. Tes yeux bizarres me suivent
when loth at landfall soft I leave.
The soldiers, Coleridge Rilke Poe,
shout commands I never heard.
They march about, dying & absurd.
Toddlers are taking over. O

ver! Sabbath belling. Snoods converge
on a weary-daring man.
What now can be cleared up? from the Yard the visitors urge.
Belle thro' the graves in a blast of sun
to the kirk moves the youngest witch.
Watch.

God bless Henry. He lived like a rat,
with a thatch of hair on his head
in the beginning.
Henry was not a coward. Much.
He never deserted anything; instead
he stuck, when things like pity were thinning.

So may be Henry was a human being.
Let's investigate that.
. . . We did; okay.
He is a human American man.
That's true. My lass is braking.
My brass is aching. Come & diminish me, & map my way.

God's Henry's enemy. We're in business . . . Why,
what business must be clear.
A cornering.
I couldn't feel more like it. —Mr Bones,
as I look on the saffron sky,
you strikes me as ornery.

Life, friends, is boring. We must not say so.
After all, the sky flashes, the great sea yearns,
we ourselves flash and yearn,
and moreover my mother told me as a boy
(repeatingly) 'Ever to confess you're bored
means you have no

Inner Resources.' I conclude now I have no
inner resources, because I am heavy bored.
Peoples bore me,
literature bores me, especially great literature,
Henry bores me, with his plights & gripes
as bad as achilles,

who loves people and valiant art, which bores me.
And the tranquil hills, & gin, look like a drag
and somehow a dog
has taken itself & its tail considerably away
into mountains or sea or sky, leaving
behind: me, wag.

Let us suppose, valleys & such ago,
one pal unwinding from his labours in
one bar of Chicago,
and this did actual happen. This was so.
And many graces are slipped, & many a sin
even that laid man low

but this will be remembered & told over,
that she was heard at last, haughtful & greasy,
to bawl in that low bar:
'You can biff me, you can bang me, get it you'll never.
I may be only a Polack     broad but I don't lay easy.
Kiss my ass, that's what you are.'

Women is better, braver. In a foehn of loss
entire, which too they hotter understand,
having had it,
we struggle. Some hang heavy on the sauce,
some invest in the past, one hides in the land.
Henry was not his favourite.

Henry's pelt was put on sundry walls
where it did much resemble Henry and
them persons was delighted.
Especially his long & glowing tail
by all them was admired, and visitors.
They whistled: This is *it*!

Golden, whilst your frozen daiquiris
whir at midnight, gleams on you his fur
& silky & black.
Mission accomplished, pal.
My molten yellow & moonless bag,
drained, hangs at rest.

Collect in the cold depths barracuda. Ay,
in Sealdah Station some possessionless
children survive to die.
The Chinese communes hum. Two daiquiris
withdrew into a corner of the gorgeous room
and one told the other a lie.

Muttered Henry:—Lord of matter, thus:
upon some more unquiet spirit knock,
my madnesses have cease.
All the quarter astonishes a lonely out & back.
They set their clocks by Henry House,
the steadiest man on the block.

And Lucifer:—I smell you for my own,
by smug. —What have I tossed you but the least
(tho' hard); fit for your ears.
Your servant, bored with horror, sat alone
with busy teeth while his dislike increased
unto himself, in tears.

And he:—O promising despair,
in solitude— —End there.
Your avenues are dying: leave me: I dove
under the oaken arms of Brother Martin,
St Simeon the Lesser Theologian,
Bodhidharma, and the Baal Shem Tov.

## *A Strut for Roethke*

Westward, hit a low note, for a roarer lost
across the Sound but north from Bremerton,
hit a way down note.
And never cadenza again of flowers, or cost.
Him who could really do that cleared his throat
& staggered on.

The bluebells, pool-shallows, saluted his over-needs,
while the clouds growled, heh-heh, & snapped, & crashed.

No stunt he'll ever unflinch once more will fail
(O lucky fellow, eh Bones?)—drifted off upstairs,
downstairs, somewheres.
No more daily, trying to hit the head on the nail:
thirstless: without a think in his head:
back from wherever, with it said.

Hit a high long note, for a lover found
needing a lower into friendlier ground
to bug among worms no more
around um jungles where ah blurt 'What for?'
Weeds, too, he favoured as      most men don't favour men.
The Garden Master's gone.

Here, whence
all have departed or will do, here airless, where
that witchy ball
wanted, fought toward, dreamed of, all a green living
drops limply into one's hands
without pleasure or interest

Figurez-vous, a time swarms when the word
'happy' sheds its whole meaning, like to come and
like for memory too
That morning arrived to Henry as well a great cheque
eaten out already by the Government & State &
other strange matters

Gentle friendly Henry Pussy-cat
smiled into his mirror, a murderer's
(at Stillwater), at himself alone
and said across a plink to that desolate fellow
said a little hail & buck-you-up
upon his triumph

# *The Secret of the Wisdom*

When worst got things, how was you? Steady on?
Wheedling, or shockt her &
you have been bad to your friend,
whom not you writing to. You have not listened.
A pelican of lies
you loosed: where are you?

Down weeks of evenings of longing
by hours, NOW, a stoned bell,
you did somebody: others you hurt short:
anyone ever did you do good?
You licking your own old hurt,
what?

An evil kneel & adore.
This is human. Hurl, God who found
us in this, down
something . . . We hear the more
sin has increast, the more
grace has been caused to abound.

Some good people, daring & subtle voices
and their tense faces, as I think of it
I see sank underground.
I see. My radar digs. I do not dig.
Cool their flushing blood, them eyes is shut—
eyes?

Appalled: by all the dead: Henry brooded.
Without exception! All.
ALL.
The senior population      waits. Come down! come down!
A ghastly & flashing pause, clothed,
life called; us do.

In a madhouse heard I an ancient man
tube-fed who had not said for fifteen years
(they said) one canny word,
senile forever, who a heart might pierce,
mutter 'O come on down. O come on down.'
Clear whom *he* meant.

# Of 1826

I am the little man who smokes & smokes.
I am the girl who does know better but.
I am the king of the pool.
I am so wise I had my mouth sewn shut.
I am a government official & a goddamned fool.
I am a lady who takes jokes.

I am the enemy of the mind.
I am the auto salesman and lóve you.
I am a teenage cancer, with a plan.
I am the blackt-out man.
I am the woman powerful as a zoo.
I am two eyes screwed to my set, whose blind—

It is the Fourth of July.
Collect: while the dying man,
forgone by you creator, who forgives,
is gasping 'Thomas Jefferson still lives'
in vain, in vain, in vain.
I am Henry Pussy-cat! My whiskers fly.

# The Lay of Ike

This is the lay of Ike.
Here's to the glory of the Great White—awk—
who has been running—er—er—things in recent—ech—
in the United—If your screen is black,
ladies & gentlemen, we—I like—
at the Point he was already terrific—sick

to a second term, having done no wrong—
no right—no right—having let the Army—bang—
defend itself from Joe, let venom' Strauss
bile Oppenheimer out of use—use Robb,
who'll later fend for Goldfine—Breaking no laws,
he lay in the White House—sob!!—

who never understood his own strategy—whee—
so Monty's memoirs—nor any strategy,
wanting the ball bulled thro' all parts of the line
at once,—proving, by his refusal to take Berlin,
he misread even Clauswitz—wide empty grin
that never lost a vote (O Adlai mine).

Oh servant Henry lectured till
the crows commenced and then
he bulbed his voice & lectured on some more.
This happened again & again, like war,—
the Indian p.a.'s, such as they were,
a weapon on his side, for the birds.

Vexations held a field-monsoon.
He was Introduced, and then he was Summed-up.
He was put questions on race bigotry;
*he* put no questions on race bigotry
constantly.
The mad sun rose though on the ghats
   & the saddhu in maha mudra, the great River,

and Henry was happy & beside him with excitement.
Beside himself, his possibilities;
salaaming hours of a half-blind morning
while the rainy lepers salaamed back,
smiles & a passion of their & his eyes flew
in feelings not ever accorded solely to oneself.

Henry, edged, decidedly, made up stories
lighting the past of Henry, of his glorious
present, and his hoaries,
all the bight heals he tamped— —Euphoria,
Mr Bones, euphoria. Fate clobber all.
—Hand me back my crawl,

condign Heaven. Tighten into a ball
elongate & valved Henry. Tuck him peace.
Render him sightless,
or ruin at high rate his crampon focus,
wipe out his need. Reduce him to the rest of us.
—But, Bones, you is that.

—I cannot remember. I am going away.
There was something in my dream about a Cat,
which fought and sang.
Something about a lyre, an island. Unstrung.
Linked to the land at low tide. Cables fray.
Thank you for everything.

The glories of the world struck me, made me aria, once.
—What happen then, Mr Bones?
if be you cares to say.
—Henry. Henry became interested in women's bodies,
his loins were & were the    scene of stupendous achievement.
Stupor. Knees, dear. Pray.

All the knobs & softnesses of, my God,
the ducking & trouble it swarm on Henry,
at one time.
—What happen then, Mr Bones?
you seems excited-like.
—Fell Henry back into    the original crime: art, rime

besides a sense of others, my God, my God,
and a jealousy for the honour (alive) of his country,
what can get more odd?
and discontent with the thriving gangs & pride.
—What happen then, Mr Bones?
—I had a most marvellous    piece of luck. I died.

**II**

The greens of the Ganges delta foliate.
Of heartless youth made late aware he pled:
Brownies, please come.
To Henry in his sparest times sometimes
the little people spread, & did friendly things;
then he was glad.

Pleased, at the worst, except with man, he shook
the brightest winter sun.
All the green lives
of the great delta, hours, hurt his migrant heart
in a safety of the steady 'plane. Please, please
come.

My friends,—he has been known to mourn,—I'll die;
live you, in the most wild, kindly, green
partly forgiving wood,
sort of forever and all those human sings
close not your better ears to, while good Spring
returns with a dance and a sigh.

## *Snow Line*

It was wet & white & swift and where I am
we don't know. It was dark and then
it isn't.
I wish the barker would come. There seems to be to eat
nothing. I am unusually tired.
I'm alone too.

If only the strange one with so few legs would come,
I'd say my prayers out of my mouth, as usual.
Where are his notes I loved?
There may be horribles; it's hard to tell.
The barker nips me but somehow I feel
he too is on my side.

I'm too alone. I see no end. If we could all
run, even that would be better. I am hungry.
The sun is not hot.
It's not a good position I am in.
If I had to do the whole thing over again
I wouldn't.

There sat down, once, a thing on Henry's heart
só heavy, if he had a hundred years
& more, & weeping, sleepless, in all them time
Henry could not make good.
Starts again always in Henry's ears
the little cough somewhere, an odour, a chime.

And there is another thing he has in mind
like a grave Sienese face a thousand years
would fail to blur the still profiled reproach of. Ghastly,
with open eyes, he attends, blind.
All the bells say: too late. This is not for tears;
thinking.

But never did Henry, as he thought he did,
end anyone and hacks her body up
and hide the pieces, where they may be found.
He knows: he went over everyone, & nobody's missing.
Often he reckons, in the dawn, them up.
Nobody is ever missing.

Collating bones: I would have liked to do.
Henry would have been hot at that.
I missed his profession.
As a little boy I always thought
'I'm an archeologist'; who
could be more respected peaceful serious than that?

Hell talkt my brain awake.
Bluffed to the ends of me pain
& I took up a pencil;
like this I'm longing with. One sign
would snow me back, back.
Is there anyone in the audience who has lived in vain?

A Chinese tooth! African jaw!
Drool, says a nervous system,
for a joyous replacing. Heat burns off dew.
Between the Ices (Mindel-Würm)
in a world I ever saw
some of my dying people indexed: "Warm."

Henry Hankovitch, con guítar,
did a short Zen pray,
on his tatami in a relaxed lotos
fixin his mind on nuffin, rose-blue breasts,
and gave his parnel one French kiss;
enslaving himself he withdrew from his blue

Florentine leather case an Egyptian black
& flickt a zippo.
Henry & Phoebe happy as cockroaches
in the world-kitchen woofed, with all away.
The international flame, like despair, rose
or like the foolish Paks or Sudanese

Henry Hankovitch, con guítar,
did a praying mantis pray
who even more obviously than the increasingly fanatical Americans
cannot govern themselves. Swedes don't exist,
Scandinavians in general do not exist,
take it from there.

And where, friend Quo, lay you hiding
across malignant half my years or so?
One evil faery
it was workt night, with amoroso pleasing
menace, the panes shake
where Lie-by-the-fire is waiting for his cream.

A tiger by a torrent in rain, wind,
narrows fiend's eyes for grief
in an old ink-on-silk,
reminding me of Delphi, and,
friend Quo, once was safe
imagination as sweet milk.

Let all flowers wither like a party.
And now you have abandoned
own your young & old, the oldest, people
to a solitudinem of mournful communes,
mournful communes.
Status, Status, come home.

An apple arc'd toward Kleitos; whose great King
wroth & of wine did study where his sword,
sneaked away, might be . . .
with swollen lids staggered up and clung
dim to the cloth of gold. An un-Greek word
blister, to him his guard,

and the trumpeter would not sound, fisted. Ha,
they hustle Clitus out; by another door,
loaded, crowds he back in
who now must, chopped, fall to the spear-ax ah
grabbed from an extra by the boy-god, sore
for weapons. For the sin:

little it is gross Henry has to say.
The King heaved. Pluckt out, the ax-end would
he jab in his sole throat.
As if an end. A baby, the guard may
squire him to his apartments. Weeping & blood
wound round his one friend.

My mother has your shotgun. One man, wide
in the mind, and tendoned like a grizzly, pried
to his trigger-digit, pal.
He should not have done that, but, I guess,
he didn't feel the best, Sister,—felt less
and more about less than us . . . ?

Now—tell me, my love, *if* you recall
the dove light after dawn at the island and all—
here is the story, Jack:
he verbed for forty years, very enough,
& shot & buckt—and, baby, there was of
schist but small there (some).

Why should I tell a truth? when in the crack
of the dooming & emptying news I did hold back—
in the taxi too, sick—
silent—it's so I broke down here, in his mind
whose sire as mine one same way— I refuse,
hoping the guy go home.

*MLA*

Hey, out there!—assistant professors, full,
associates,—instructors—others—any—
I have a sing to shay.
We are assembled here in the capital
city for Dull—and one professor's wife is Mary—
at Christmastide, hey!

and all of you did theses or are doing
and the moral history of what we were up to
thrives in Sir Wilson's hands—
who I don't see here—only deals go screwing
some of you out, some up—the chairmen too
are nervous, little friends—

a chairman's not a chairman, son, forever,
and hurts with his appointments; ha, but circle—
take my word for it—
though maybe Frost is dying—around Mary;
forget your footnotes on the old gentleman;
dance around Mary.

The high ones die, die. They die. You look up and who's there?
—Easy, easy, Mr Bones. I is on your side.
I smell your grief.
—I sent my grief away. I cannot care
forever. With them all again & again I died
and cried, and I have to live.

—Now there *you* exaggerate, Sah. We hafta *die.*
That is our 'pointed task. Love & die.
—Yes; that makes sense.
But what makes sense between, then? What if I
roiling & babbling & braining, brood on why and
just sat on the fence?

—I doubts you did or do. De choice is lost.
—It's fool's gold. But I go in for that.
The boy & the bear
looked at each other. Man all is tossed
& lost with groin-wounds by the grand bulls, cat.
William Faulkner's where?

(Frost being still around.)

40

# Three around the Old Gentleman

His malice was a pimple down his good
big face, with its sly eyes. I must be sorry
Mr Frost has left:
I like it so less I don't understood—
he couldn't hear or see well—all we sift—
but this is a *bad* story.

He had fine stories and was another man
in private; difficult, always. Courteous,
on the whole, in private.
He apologize to Henry, off & on,
for two blue slanders; which was good of him.
I don't know how he made it.

Quickly, off stage with all but kindness, now.
I can't say what I have in mind. Bless Frost,
any odd god around.
Gentle his shift, I decussate & command,
stoic deity. For a while here we possessed
an unusual man.

The Russian grin bellows his condolence
tó the family: ah but it's Kay,
& Ted, & Chis & Anne,
Henry thinks of: who eased his fearful way
from here, in here, to there. This wants thought.
I won't make it out.

Maybe the source of noble such may come
clearer to dazzled Henry. It may come.
I'd say it will come with pain,
in mystery. I'd rather leave it alone.
I do leave it alone.
And down with the listener.

Now he has become, abrupt, an industry.
Professional-Friends-Of-Robert-Frost all over
gap wide their mouths
while the quirky medium of so many truths
is quiet. Let's be quiet. Let us listen:
—What for, Mr Bones?
        —while he begins to have it out with Horace.

Goodbye, sir, & fare well. You're in the clear.
'Nobody' (Mark says    you said) 'is ever found out.'
I figure you were right,
having as Henry got away with murder
for long. Some jarred clock tell me it's late,
not for you who went straight

but for the lorn. Our roof is lefted off
lately: the shooter, and the bourbon man,
and then you got tired.
I'm afraid that's it. I figure you with love,
lifey, deathy, but I have a little sense
the rest of us are fired

or fired: be with us: we will blow our best,
our sad wild riffs come easy in that case,
thinking you over,
knowing you resting, who was reborn to rest,
your gorgeous sentence done. Nothing's the same,
sir,—taking cover.

I'm scared a lonely. Never see my son,
easy be not to see anyone,
combers out to sea
know they're goin somewhere but not me.
Got a little poison, got a little gun,
I'm scared a lonely.

I'm scared a only one thing, which is me,
from othering I don't take nothin, see,
for any hound dog's sake.
But this is where I livin, where I rake
my leaves and cop my promise, this' where we
cry oursel's awake.

Wishin was dyin but I gotta make
it all this way to that bed on these feet
where peoples said to meet.
Maybe but even if I see my son
forever never, get back on the take,
free, black & forty-one.

If we sang in the wood (and Death is a German expert)
while snows flies, chill, after so frequent knew
so many all of nothing,
for lead & fire, it's not we would assert
particulars, but animal; cats mew,
horses scream, man sing.

Or: men psalm. Man palms his ears and moans.
Death is a German expert. Scrambling, sitting,
spattering, we hurry.
I try to. Odd & trivial, atones
somehow for *my* escape a bullet splitting
my trod-on instep, fiery.

The cantor bubbled, rattled. The Temple burned.
Lurch with me! phantoms of Varshava. Slop!
When I used to be,
who haunted, stumbling, sewers, my sacked shop,
roofs, a dis-world *ai!* Death was a German
home-country.

O journeyer, deaf in the mould, insane
with violent travel & death: consider me
in my cast, your first son.
Would you were I by now another one,
witted, legged? I see you before me plain
(I am skilled: I hear, I see)—

your honour was troubled: when you wondered—'No'.
I hear. I think I hear. Now full craze down
across our continent
all storms since you gave in, on my pup-tent.
I have of blast & counter to remercy you
for hurling me downtown.

We dream of honour, and we get along.
Fate winged me, in the person of a cab
and your stance on the sand.
Think it across, in freezing wind: withstand
my blistered wish: flop, there, to his blind song
who pick up the tab.

'Oyez, oyez!' The Man Who Did Not Deliver
is before you for his deliverance, my lords.
*He stands, as charged*
for This by banks, That cops, by lawyers, by
publishingers for Them. I doubt he'll make
old bones.

Be.
I warned him, of a summer night: consist,
consist. Ex-wives roar.
Further, the Crown holds that they spilt himself,
splitting his manward chances, to his shame,
my lords, & our horror.

Behind, oh worst lean backward them who bring
un-charges: hundreds & one, children,
the pillars & the sot.
Henry thought. It is so. I must sting.
Listen! the grave ground-rhythm of a gone
. . . makar? So what.

Tell it to the forest fire, tell it to the moon,
mention it in general to the moon
on the way down,
he's about to have his lady, permanent;
and this is the worst of all came ever sent
writhing Henry's way.

Ha ha, fifth column, quisling, genocide,
he held his hands & laught from side to side
a loverly time.
The berries & the rods left him alone less.
Thro' a race of water once I went: happiness.
I'll walk into the sky.

There the great flare & stench, O flying creatures,
surely will dim-dim? Bars will be closed.
No girl will again
conceive above your throes. A fine thunder peals
will with its friends and soon, from agony
put the fire out.

He stared at ruin. Ruin stared straight back.
He thought they was old friends. He felt on the stair
where her papa found them bare
they became familiar. When the papers were lost
rich with pals' secrets, he thought he had the knack
of ruin. Their paths crossed

and once they crossed in jail; they crossed in bed;
and over an unsigned letter their eyes met,
and in an Asian city
directionless & lurchy at two & three,
or trembling to a telephone's fresh threat,
and when some wired his head

to reach a wrong opinion, 'Epileptic'.
But he noted now that: they were not old friends.
He did not know this one.
This one was a stranger, come to make amends
for all the imposters, and to make it stick.
Henry nodded, un-.

# 4 6

I am, outside. Incredible panic rules.
People are blowing and beating each other without mercy.
Drinks are boiling. Iced
drinks are boiling. The worse anyone feels, the worse
treated he is. Fools elect fools.
A harmless man at an intersection said, under his breath: "Christ!"

That word, so spoken, affected the vision
of, when they trod to work next day, shopkeepers
who went & were fitted for glasses.
Enjoyed they then an appearance of love & law.
Millenia whift & waft—one, one—er, er . . .
Their glasses were taken from them, & they saw.

Man has undertaken the top job of all,
*son fin*. Good luck.
I myself walked at the funeral of tenderness.
Followed other deaths. Among the last,
like the memory of a lovely fuck,
was: *Do, ut des*.

# April Fool's Day, or, St Mary of Egypt

—Thass a funny title, Mr Bones.
—When down she saw her feet, sweet fish, on the threshold,
she considered her fair shoulders
and all them hundreds who have held them, all
the more who to her mime thickened & maled
from the supple stage,

and seeing her feet, in a visit, side by side
paused on the sill of The Tomb, she shrank: 'No.
They are not worthy,
fondled by many' and rushed from The Crucified
back through her followers out of the city ho
across the suburbs, plucky

to dare my desert in her late daylight
of animals and sands. She fall prone.
Only wind whistled.
And forty-seven years went by like Einstein.
We celebrate her feast with our caps on,
whom God has not visited.

He yelled at me in Greek,
my God!—It's not his language
and I'm no good at—his is Aramaic,
was—I am a monoglot of English
(American version) and, say pieces from
a baker's dozen others: where's the bread?

but rising in the Second Gospel, pal:
The seed goes down, god dies,
a rising happens,
some crust, and then occurs     an eating. He said so,
a Greek idea,
troublesome to imaginary Jews,

like bitter Henry, full of the death of love,
Cawdor-uneasy, disambitious, mourning
the whole implausible necessary thing.
He dropped his voice & sybilled of
the death of the death of love.
I óught to get going.

# Blind

Old Pussy-cat if he won't eat, he don't
feel good into his tum', old Pussy-cat.
He *wants* to have eaten.
Tremor, heaves, he sweaterings. He can't.
A dizzy swims of where is Henry at;
. . . somewhere streng verboten.

How come he sleeps & sleeps and sleeps, waking like death:
locate the restorations of which we hear
as of profound sleep.
From daylight he got maintrackt, from friends' breath,
wishes, his hopings. Dreams make crawl with fear
Henry but not get up.

The course his mind his body steer, poor Pussy-cat,
in weakness & disorder, will see him down
whiskers & tail.
'Wastethrift': Oh one of cunning wives know that
he hoardy-squander, where is nor downtown
neither suburba. Braille.

In a motion of night they massed nearer my post.
I hummed a short blues. When the stars went out
I studied my weapons system.
Grenades, the portable rack, the yellow spout
of the anthrax-ray: in order. Yes, and most
of my pencils were sharp.

This edge of the galaxy has often seen
a defence so stiff, but it could only go
one way.
—Mr Bones, your troubles give me vertigo,
& backache. Somehow, when I make your scene,
I cave to feel as if

de roses of dawns & pearls of dusks, made up
by some ol' writer-man, got right forgot
& the greennesses of ours.
Springwater grow so thick it gonna clot
and the pleasing ladies cease. I figure, yup,
you is bad powers.

Our wounds to time, from all the other times,
sea-times slow, the times of galaxies
fleeing, the dwarfs' dead times,
lessen so little that if here in his crude rimes
Henry them mentions, do not hold it, please,
for a putting of man down.

Ol' Marster, being bound you do your best
versus we coons, spare now a cagey John
a whilom bits that whip:
who'll tell your fortune, when you have confessed
whose & whose woundings—against the innocent stars
& remorseless seas—

—Are you radioactive, pal? —Pal, radioactive.
—Has you the night sweats & the day sweats, pal?
—Pal, I do.
—Did your gal leave you? —What do *you* think, pal?
—Is that thing on the front of your head what it seems to be, pal?
—Yes, pal.

# III

# 5 2

## *Silent Song*

Bright-eyed & bushy-tailed woke not Henry up.
Bright though upon his workshop shone a vise
central, moved in
while he was doing time down hospital
and growing wise.
He gave it the worst look he had left.

Alone. They all abandoned      Henry—wonder! all,
when most he—under the sun.
That was all right.
He can't work well with it here, or think.
A bilocation, yellow like catastrophe.
The name of this was freedom.

Will Henry again ever be on the lookout for women & milk,
honour & love again,
have a buck or three?
He felt like shrieking but he shuddered as
(spring mist, warm, rain) an handful with quietness
vanisht & the thing took hold.

He lay in the middle of the world, and twitcht.
More Sparine for Pelides,
human (half) & down here as he is,
with probably insulting mail to open
and certainly unworthy words to hear
and his unforgivable memory.

—I seldom *go* to *films*. They are too exciting,
said the Honourable Possum.
—It takes me so long to read the 'paper,
said to me one day a novelist hot as a firecracker,
because I have to identify myself with everyone in it,
including the corpses, pal.'

Kierkegaard wanted a society, to refuse to read 'papers,
and that was not, friends, his worst idea.
Tiny Hardy, toward the end, refused to say *anything*,
a programme adopted early on by long Housman,
and Gottfried Benn
said:—We are using our own skins for wallpaper and we cannot win.

'NO VISITORS' I thumb the roller to
and leans against the door.
Comfortable in my horseblanket
I prop on the costly bed & dream of my wife,
my first wife,
and my second wife & my son.

Insulting, they put guardrails up,
as if it were a crib!
I growl at the head nurse; we compose on one.
I have been operating from *nothing*,
like a dog after its tail
more slowly, losing altitude.

Nitid. They are shooting me full of sings.
I give no rules. Write as short as you can,
in order, of what matters.
I think of my beloved poet
Issa & his father who
sat down on the grass and took leave of each other.

Peter's not friendly. He gives me sideways looks.
The architecture is far from reassuring.
I feel uneasy.
A pity,—the interview began so well:
I mentioned fiendish things, he waved them away
and sloshed out a martini

strangely needed. We spoke of indifferent matters—
God's health, the vague hell of the Congo,
John's energy,
anti-matter matter. I felt fine.
Then a change came backward. A chill fell.
Talk slackened,

died, and he began to give me sideways looks.
'Christ,' I thought 'what now?' and would have askt for another
but didn't dare.
I feel my application     failing. It's growing dark,
some other sound is overcoming. His last words are:
'We betrayed me.'

Hell is empty. O that has come to pass
which the cut Alexandrian foresaw,
and Hell lies empty.
Lightning fell silent where the Devil knelt
and over the whole grave space hath settled awe
in a full death of guilt.

The tinchel closes. Terror, & plunging, swipes.
I lay my ears back. I am about to die.
My cleft feet drum.
Fierce, the two-footers club. My green world pipes
a finish—for us all, my love, not some.
Crumpling, I—why,—

So in his crystal ball them two he weighs,
solidly, dreaming of his sleepy son,
ah him, and his new wife.
What roar solved once the dilemma of the Ancient of Days,
what sigh borrowed His mercy?—Who may, if
we are all the same, make one.

In a state of chortle sin—once he reflected,
swilling tomato juice—live I, and did
more than my thirstier years.
To Hell then will it maul me? for good talk,
and gripe of retail loss? I dare say not.
I don't think there's that place

save sullen here, wherefrom she flies tonight
retrieving her whole body, which I need.
I recall a 'coon treed,
flashlights, & barks, and I was in that tree,
and something can (has) been said for sobriety
but very little.

The guns. Ah, darling, it was late for me,
midnight, at seven. How in famished youth
could I foresee Henry's sweet seed
unspent across so flying barren ground,
where would my loves dislimn whose dogs abound?
I fell out of the tree.

Industrious, affable, having brain on fire,
Henry perplexed himself; others gave up;
good girls gave in;
geography was hard on friendship, Sire;
marriages lashed & languished, anguished; dearth of group
and what else had been;

the splendour & the lose grew all the same,
Sire. His heart stiffened, and he failed to smile,
catching *(enfint)* on.
The law: we must, owing to chiefly shame
lacing our pride, down what we did. A mile,
a mile to Avalon.

Stuffy & lazy, shaky, making roar
overseas presses, he quit wondering:
the mystery is full.
Sire, damp me down. Me feudal O, me yore
(male Muse) serf, if anyfing;
which rank I pull.

# Henry's Meditation in the Kremlin

Down on the cathedrals, as from the Giralda
in a land no crueller, and over the walls
to domes & river look
from Great John's belfry, Ivan-Veliky,
whose thirty-one are still
to hail who storms no father's throne. Bell, book

& candle rule, in silence. Hour by hour
from time to time with holy oil
touch yet the forehead eyelids nose
lips ears breast fists of Krushchev, for Christ knows
poor evil Kadar, cut, is back in power.
Boils his throne. The moujik kneels & votes.

South & east of the others' tombs—where? why,
in Arkhanghelsky, on the Baptist's side,
lies Brother Jonas (formerly Ivan the Terrible),
where Brother Josef came with his fiend's heart
out of such guilt it proved all bearable,
and Brother Nikita will come and lie.

Afters eight years, be less dan eight percent,
distinguish' friend, of coloured wif de whites
in de School, in de Souf.
—Is coloured gobs, is coloured officers,
Mr Bones. Dat's nuffin? —Uncle Tom,
sweep shut yo mouf,

is million blocking from de proper job,
de fairest houses & de churches eben.
—You may be right, Friend Bones.
Indeed you is. Dey flyin ober de world,
de pilots, ober ofays. Bit by bit
our immemorial moans

brown down to all dere moans. I flees that, sah.
They brownin up to ourn. Who gonna win?
—I wouldn't *pre*dict.
But I do guess mos peoples gonna *lose*.
I never saw no pinkie wifout no hand.
O my, without no hand.

Full moon. Our Narragansett gales subside
and the land is celebrating men of war
more or less, less or more.
In valleys, thin on headlands, narrow & wide
our targets rest. In us we trust. Far, near,
the bivouacs of fear

are solemn in the moon somewhere tonight,
in turning time. It's late for gratitude,
an annual, rude
roar of a moment's turkey's 'Thanks'. Bright & white
their ordered markers undulate away
awaiting no day.

Away from us, from Henry's feel or fail,
campaigners lie with mouldered toes, disarmed,
out of order,
with whom we will one. The war is real,
and a sullen glory pauses over them harmed,
incident to murder.

That dark brown rabbit, lightness in his ears
& underneath, gladdened our afternoon
munching a crab-'.
That rabbit was a fraud, like a black bull
*prudent* I admired in Zaragoza, who
certainly was brave as a demon

but would not charge, being willing not to die.
The rabbit's case, a little different,
consisted in alert
& wily looks down the lawn, where nobody was,
with prickt ears, while rapt but chatting on the porch
we sat in view nearby.

Then went he mildly by, and around behind
my cabin, and when I followed, there he just sat.
Only at last
he turned down around, passing my wife at four feet
and hopped the whole lawn and made thro' the hedge for the big
  house.
—Mr Bones, we all brutes & fools.

Bats have no bankers and they do not drink
and cannot be arrested and pay no tax
and, in general, bats have it made.
Henry for joining the human race is *bats*,
known to be so, by few them who think,
out of the cave.

Instead of the cave! ah lovely-chilly, dark,
ur-moist his cousins hang in hundreds or swerve
with personal radar,
crisisless, kid. Instead of the cave? I serve,
inside, my blind term. Filthy four-foot lights
reflect on the whites of our eyes.

He then salutes for sixty years of it
just now a one of valor and insights,
a theatrical man,
O scholar & Legionnaire who as quickly might
have killed as cast you. *Olè*. Stormed with years
he tranquil commands and appears.

Supreme my holdings, greater yet my need,
thoughtless I go out.     Dawn.     Have I my cig's,
my flaskie O,
O crystal cock,—my kneel has gone to seed,—
and anybody's blessing? (Blast the MIGs
for making fumble so

my tardy readying.) Yes, utter' that.
Anybody's blessing? —Mr Bones,
you makes too much
démand. I might be 'fording you a hat:
it gonna rain. —I knew a one of groans
& greed & spite, of a crutch,

who thought he had, a vile night, been—well—blest.
He see someone run off. Why not Henry,
with his grasp of desire?
—Hear matters hard to manage at de best,
Mr Bones. Tween what we see, what be,
is blinds. Them blinds' on fire.

A freaking ankle crabbed his blissful trips,
this whisky tastes like California
but is Kentucky,
like Berkeley where he truly worked at it
but nothing broke all night—no fires—one dawn,
crowding his luck,

flowed down along the cliffs to the Big Sur
where Henry Miller's box is vomit-green
and Henry bathed in sulphur
lovely, hot, over the sea, like Senator
Cat, relaxed & sober, watery
as Tivoli, sir.

No Christmas jaunts for fractured cats. Hot dog,
the world is places where he will not go
this wintertide or again.
Does Striding Edge block wild the sky as then
when Henry with his mystery was two
& twenty, high on the hog?

'All virtues enter into this world:')
A Buddhist, doused in the street, serenely burned.
The Secretary of State for War,
winking it over, screwed a redhaired whore.
Monsignor Capovilla mourned. What a week.
A journalism doggy took a leak

against absconding coon ('but take one virtue,
without which a man can hardly hold his own')
the sun in the willow
shivers itself & shakes itself green-yellow
(Abba Pimen groaned, over the telephone,
when asked what that was:)

How feel a fellow then when he arrive
in fame but lost? but affable, top-shelf.
Quelle sad semaine.
He hardly know his selving. ('that a man')
Henry grew hot, got laid, felt bad, survived
('should always reproach himself'.

# 6 7

I don't operate often. When I do,
persons take note.
Nurses look amazed. They pale.
The patient is brought back to life, or so.
The reason I don't do this more (I quote)
is: I have a living to fail—

because of my wife & son—to keep from earning.
—Mr Bones, I sees that.
They for these operations thanks you, what?
not pays you. —Right.
You have seldom been so understanding.
Now there is further a difficulty with the light:

I am obliged to perform in complete darkness
operations of great delicacy
on my self.
—Mr Bones, you terrifies me.
No wonder they don't pay you. Will you die?
—My
                friend, I succeeded. Later.

I heard, could be, a Hey there from the wing,
and I went on: Miss Bessie soundin good
that one, that night of all,
I feelin fair mysef, taxes & things
seem to be back in line, like everybody should
and nobody in the snow on call

so, as I say, the house is givin hell
to *Yellow Dog*, I blowin like it too
and Bessie always do
when she make a very big sound—after, well,
no sound—I see she totterin—I cross which stage
even at Henry's age

in 2-3 seconds: then we wait and see.
I hear strange horns, Pinetop he hit some chords,
Charlie start *Empty Bed*,
they all come hangin Christmas on some tree
after trees thrown out—sick-house's white birds',
black to the birds instead.

Love her he doesn't but the thought he puts
into that young woman
would launch a national product
complete with TV spots & skywriting
outlets in Bonn & Tokyo
I mean it

Let it be known that nine words have not passed
between herself and Henry;
looks, smiles.
God help Henry, who deserves it all
every least part of that infernal & unconscious
woman, and the pain.

I feel as if, unique, she . . . Biddable?
Fates, conspire.
—Mr Bones, *please.*
—Vouchsafe me, Sleepless One,
a personal experience of the body of Mrs Boogry
before I pass from lust!

Disengaged, bloody, Henry rose from the shell
where in their racing start his seat got wedged
under his knifing knees,
he did it on the runners, feathering,
being bow, catching no crab. The ridges were sore
& tore chamois. It was not done with ease.

So Henry was a hero, malgré lui,
that day, for blundering; until & after the coach
said this & which to him.
That happy day, whenas the pregnant back
of Number Two returned, and he'd no choice
but to make for it room.

Therefore he rowed rowed rowed. They did not win.
Forever in the winning & losing since
of his own crew, or rather
in the weird regattas of this afterworld,
cheer for the foe. He set himself to time
the blue father.

Spellbound held subtle Henry all his four
hearers in the racket of the market
with ancient signs, infamous characters,
new rhythms. On the steps he was beloved,
hours a day, by all his four, or more,
depending. And they paid him.

It was not, so, like no one listening
but critics famed & Henry's pals or other
tellers at all
chiefly in another country. No.
He by the heart & brains & tail, because
of their love for it, had them.

Junk he said to all them open-mouthed.
Weather wóuld govern. When the monsoon spread
its floods, few came, two.
Came a day when none, though he began
in his accustomed way on the filthy steps
in a crash of waters, came.

## The Elder Presences

Shh! on a twine hung from disastered trees
Henry is swinging his daughter. They seem drunk.
Over across them look out,
tranquil, the high statues of the wise.
Her feet peep, like a lady's in sleep sunk.
That which this scene's about—

he pushes violent, his calves distend,
his mouth is open with effort, so is hers,
in the Supreme Court garden,
the justices lean, negro, out, the trees bend,
man's try began too long ago, with chirrs
& leapings, begging pardon—

I will deny the gods of the garden say.
Henry's perhaps to break his burnt-cork luck.
I further will deny
good got us up that broad shoreline. Greed may
like a fuse, but with the high shore we is stuck,
whom they overlook. Why,—

# Karesansui, Ryoan-ji

The taxi makes the vegetables fly.
'Dozo kudasai,' I have him wait.
Past the bright lake up into the temple,
shoes off, and
my right leg swings me left.
I do survive beside the garden I

came seven thousand mile the other way
supplied of engines all to see, to see.
Differ them photographs, plans lie:
how big it is!
austere a sea rectangular     of sand by the oiled mud wall,
and the sand is not quite white: granite sand, grey,

—from nowhere can one see *all* the stones—
but helicopters or     a Brooklyn reproduction
will fix that—

and the fifteen changeless stones in their five worlds
with a shelving of moving moss
stand me the thought of the ancient maker priest.
Elsewhere occurs—I remembers—loss.
Through awes & weathers neither it increased
nor did one blow of all his stone & sand thought die.

Henry hates the world. What the world to Henry
did will not bear thought.
Feeling no pain,
Henry stabbed his arm and wrote a letter
explaining how bad it had been
in this world.

Old yellow, in a gown
might have made a difference, 'these lower beauties',
and chartreuse could have mattered

"Kyoto, Toledo,
Benares—the holy cities—
and Cambridge shimmering do not make up
for, well, the horror of unlove,
nor south from Paris driving in the Spring
to Siena and on . . ."

Pulling together Henry, somber Henry
woofed at things.
Spry disappointments of men
and vicing adorable children
miserable women, Henry mastered, Henry
tasting all the secret bits of life.

Turning it over, considering, like a madman
Henry put forth a book.
No harm resulted from this.
Neither the menstruating    stars (nor man) was moved
at once.
Bare dogs drew closer for a second look

and performed their friendly operations there.
Refreshed, the bark rejoiced.
Seasons went and came.
Leaves fell, but only a few.
Something remarkable about this
unshedding bulky bole-proud blue-green moist

thing made by savage & thoughtful
surviving Henry
began to strike the passers from despair
so that sore on their shoulders old men hoisted
six-foot sons and polished women called
small girls to dream awhile toward the flashing & bursting
    tree!

# 76

## Henry's Confession

Nothin very bad happen to me lately.
How you explain that? —I explain that, Mr Bones,
terms o' your bafflin odd sobriety.
Sober as man can get, no girls, no telephones,
what could happen bad to Mr Bones?
—*If* life is a handkerchief sandwich,

in a modesty of death I join my father
who dared so long agone leave me.
A bullet on a concrete stoop
close by a smothering southern sea
spreadeagled on an island, by my knee.
—You is from hunger, Mr Bones,

I offers you this handkerchief, now set
your left foot by my right foot,
shoulder to shoulder, all that jazz,
arm in arm, by the beautiful sea,
hum a little, Mr Bones.
—I saw nobody coming, so I went instead.

Seedy Henry rose up shy in de world
& shaved & swung his barbells, duded Henry up
and p.a.'d poor thousands of persons on topics of grand
moment to Henry, ah to those less & none.
Wif a book of his in either hand
he is stript down to move on.

—Come away, Mr Bones.

—Henry is tired of the winter,
& haircuts, & a squeamish comfy     ruin-prone proud national
    mind,     & Spring (in the city so called).
Henry likes Fall.
Hé would be prepared to líve in a world of Fáll
for ever, impenitent Henry.
But the snows and summers grieve & dream;

thése fierce & airy occupations, and love,
raved away so many of Henry's years
it is a wonder that, with in each hand
one of his own mad books and all,
ancient fires for eyes, his head full
& his heart full, he's making ready to move on.

*HIS TOY,*
*HIS DREAM,*
*HIS REST*

*To Mark Van Doren,*
*and to the sacred memory*
*of Delmore Schwartz*

NO INTERESTING PROJECT CAN BE EMBARKED ON WITHOUT
FEAR. I SHALL BE SCARED TO DEATH HALF THE TIME.

*Sir Francis Chichester in Sydney*

FOR MY PART I AM ALWAYS FRIGHTENED, AND VERY MUCH
SO. I FEAR THE FUTURE OF ALL ENGAGEMENTS.

*Gordon in Khartoum*

I AM PICKT UP AND SORTED TO A PIP. MY IMAGINATION IS
A MONASTERY AND I AM ITS MONK.

*Keats to Shelley*

HE WENT AWAY AND NEVER SAID GOODBYE.
I COULD READ HIS LETTERS BUT I SURE CAN'T READ HIS MIND.
I THOUGHT HE'S LOVIN ME BUT HE WAS LEAVIN ALL THE TIME.
NOW I KNOW THAT MY TRUE LOVE WAS BLIND.

*Victoria Spivey?*

**IV**

## Op. posth. no. 1

Darkened his eye, his wild smile disappeared,
inapprehensible his studies grew,
nourished he less & less
his subject body with good food & rest,
something bizarre about Henry, slowly sheared
off, unlike you & you,

smaller & smaller, till in question stood
his eyeteeth and one block of memories
These were enough for him
implying commands from upstairs & from down,
Walt's 'orbic flex,' triads of Hegel would
incorporate, if you please,

into the know-how of the American bard
embarrassed Henry heard himself a-being,
and the younger Stephen Crane
of a powerful memory, of pain,
these stood the ancestors, relaxed & hard,
whilst Henry's parts were fleeing.

# Op. posth. no. 2

Whence flew the litter whereon he was laid?
Of what heroic stuff was warlock Henry made?
and questions of that sort
perplexed the bulging cosmos, O in short
was sandalwood in good supply when he
flared out of history

& the obituary in *The New York Times*
into the world of generosity
creating the air where are
& can be, only, heroes? Statues & rhymes
signal his fiery Passage, a mountainous sea,
the occlusion of a star:

anything afterward, of high lament,
let too his giant faults appear, as sent
together with his virtues down
and let this day be his, throughout the town,
region & cosmos, lest he freeze our blood
with terrible returns.

# Op. posth. no.. 3

It's buried at a distance, on my insistence, buried.
Weather's severe there, which it will not mind.
I miss it.
O happies before & during & between the times it got married.
I hate the love of leaving it behind,
deteriorating & hopeless that.

The great Uh climbed above me, far above me,
doing the north face, or behind it. Does He love me?
over, & flout.
Goodness is bits of outer God. The house-guest
(slimmed-down) with one eye open & one breast
out.

Slimmed-down from by-blow; adoptive-up; was white.
A daughter of a friend. His soul is a sight.
—Mr Bones, what's all about?
Girl have a little: what be wrong with *that?*
Yóu free? —Down some many did descend
from the abominable & semi-mortal Cat.

# *Op. posth. no. 4*

He loom' so cagey he say 'Leema beans'
and measured his intake to the atmosphere
of that fairly stable country.
His ear hurt. Left. The rock-cliffs, a mite sheer
at his age, in these places.
Scrubbing out his fear,—

the knowledge that they will take off your hands,
both hands; as well as your both feet, & likewise
both eyes,
might be discouraging to a bloody hero
Also you stifle, like you can't draw breath.
But this is death—

which in some vain strive many to avoid,
many. It's on its way, where you drop at
who stood up, scrunch down small.
It wasn't so much after all to lose, was, Boyd?
A body.—But, Mr Bones, you needed that.
Now I put on my tall hat.

# Op. posth. no. 5

Maskt as honours, insult like behaving
missiles homes. I bow, & grunt 'Thank you.
I'm glad you could come
so late.' All loves are gratified. I'm having
to screw a little thing I have to screw.
Good nature is over.

Herewith ill-wishes. From a cozy grave
rainbow I scornful laughings. Do not do,
Father, me down.
Let's shuck an obligation. O I have
done. Is the inner-coffin burning blue
or did Jehovah frown?

Jehovah. Period. Yahweh. Period. God.
It is marvellous that views so differay
(Father is a Jesuit)
can love so well each other. We was had.
O visit in my last tomb me. —Perché?
—Is a *nice* pit.

# *Op. posth. no. 6*

I recall a boil, whereupon as I had to sit,
just where, and when I had to, for deadlines.
O I could learn to type standing,
but isn't it slim to be slumped off from that,
problems undignified, fiery dig salt mines?—
Content on one's back flat:

coming no deadline—is all ancient nonsense—
no typewriters—ha! ha!—no typewriters—
alas!
For I have much to open, I know immense
troubles & wonders to their secret curse.
Yet when erect on my ass,

pissed off, I sat two-square, I kept shut his mouth
and stilled my nimble fingers across keys.
That is I stood up.
Now since down I lay, void of love & ruth,
I'd howl my knowings, only there's the earth
overhead. Plop!

# Op. posth. no. 7

Plop, plop. The lobster toppled in the pot,
fulfilling, dislike man, his destiny,
glowing fire-red,
succulent, and on the whole becoming what
man wants. I crack my final claw singly,
wind up the grave, & to bed.

—Sound good, Mr Bones. I wish I had me some.
(I spose you got a lessen up your slave.)
—O no no no.
Sole I remember; where no lobster swine,—
pots hot or cold is none. With you I grieve
lightly, and I have no lesson.

Bodies are relishy, they say. Here's mine,
was. What ever happened to Political Economy,
leaving me here?
Is a rare—in my opinion—responsibility.
The military establishments perpetuate themselves forever.
Have a bite, for a sign.

# Op. posth. no. 8

Flak. An eventful thought came to me,
who squirm in my hole. How will the matter end?
Who's king these nights?
What happened to . . . day? Are ships abroad?
I would like to but may not entertain a friend.
Save me from ghastly frights,

Triune! My wood or word seems to be rotting.
I daresay I'm collapsing. Worms are at hand.
No, all that froze,
I mean the blood. 'O get up & go in'
somewhere once I heard. Nowadays I doze.
It's cold here.

The cold is ultimating. The cold is cold.
I am—I should be held together by—
but I am breaking up
and Henry now has come to a full stop—
vanisht his vision, if there was, & fold
him over himself quietly.

# Op. posth. no. 9

The conclusion is growing . . . I feel sure, my lord,
this august court will entertain the plea
Not Guilty by reason of death.
I can say no more except that for the record
I add that all the crimes since all the times he
died will be due to the breath

of unknown others, sweating in their guilt
while my client Henry's brow of stainless steel
rests free, as well it may,
of all such turbulence, whereof not built
Henry lies clear as any onion-peel
in any sandwich, say.

He spiced us: there, my lord, the wicked fault
lodges: we judged him when we did not know
and we did judge him wrong,
lying incapable of crime save salt
preservative in cases here below
adduced. Not to prolong

## Op. posth. no. 10

these hearings endlessly, friends, word is had
Henry may be returning to our life
adult & difficult.
There exist rumours that remote & sad
and quite beyond the knowledge of his wife
to the foothills of the cult

will come in silence this distinguished one
essaying once again the lower slopes
in triumph, keeping up our hopes,
and heading not for the highest we have done
but enigmatic faces, unsurveyed,
calm as a forest glade

for him. I only speak of what I hear
and I have said too much. He may be there
or he may groan in hospital
resuming, as the fates decree, our lot.
I would not interrupt him in whatever, in what
he's bracing him to at all.

# Op. posth. no. 11

In slack times visit I the violent dead
and pick their awful brains. Most seem to feel
nothing is secret more
to my disdain I find, when we who fled
cherish the knowings of both worlds, conceal
more, beat on the floor,

where Bhain is stagnant, dear of Henry's friends,
yellow with cancer, paper-thin, & bent
even in the hospital bed
racked with high hope, on whom death lay hands
in weeks, or Yeats in the London spring half-spent,
only the grand gift in his head

going for him, a seated ruin of a man
courteous to a junior, like one of the boarders,
or Dylan, with more to say
now there's no hurry, and we're all a clan.
You'd think off here one would be free from orders.
I didn't hear a single      word. I obeyed.

# *Op. posth. no. 12*

In a blue series towards his sleepy eyes
they slid like wonder, women tall & small,
of every shape & size,
in many languages to lisp 'We do'
to Henry almost waking. What is the night at all,
his closed eyes beckon you.

In the Marriage of the Dead, a new routine,
he gasped his crowded vows past lids shut tight
and a-many rings fumbled on.
His coffin like Grand Central to the brim
filled up & emptied with the lapse of light.
Which one will waken him?

O she must startle like a fallen gown,
content with speech like an old sacrament
in deaf ears lying down,
blazing through darkness till he feels the cold
& blindness of his hopeless tenement
while his black arms unfold.

# Op. posth. no. 13

In the night-reaches dreamed he of better graces,
of liberations, and beloved faces,
such as now ere dawn he sings.
It would not be easy, accustomed to these things,
to give up the old world, but he could try;
let it all rest, have a good cry.

Let Randall rest, whom your self-torturing
cannot restore one instant's good to, rest:
he's left us now.
The panic died and in the panic's dying
so did my old friend. I am headed west
also, also, somehow.

In the chambers of the end we'll meet again
I will say Randall, he'll say Pussycat
and all will be as before
whenas we sought, among the beloved faces,
eminence and were dissatisfied with that
and needed more.

# *Op. posth. no. 14*

Noises from underground made gibber some
others collected & dug Henry up
saying 'You *are* a sight.'
Chilly, he muttered for a double rum
waving the mikes away, putting a stop
to rumours, pushing his fright

off with the now accumulated taxes
accustomed in his way to solitude
and no bills.
Wives came forward, claiming a new Axis,
fearful for their insurance, though, now, glued
to disencumbered Henry's many ills.

A fortnight later, sense a single man
upon the trampled scene at 2 a.m.
insomnia-plagued, with a shovel
digging like mad, Lazarus with a plan
to get his own back, a plan, a stratagem
no newsman will unravel.

**V**

# Room 231: the forth week

Something black somewhere    in the vistas of his heart.

Tulips from Tates teazed Henry in the mood
to be a tulip and desire no more
but water, but light, but air.
Yet his nerves rattled blackly, unsubdued,
& suffocation called, dream-whiskey'd pour
sirening. Rosy there

too fly my Phil & Ellen roses, pal.
Flesh-coloured men & women come & punt
under my windows. I rave
or grunt against it, from a flowerless land.
For timeless hours wind most, or not at all. I wind
my clock before I shave.

Soon it will fall dark. Soon you'll see stars
you fevered after, child, man, & did nothing,—
compass live to the pencil-torch!
As still as his cadaver, Henry mars
this surface of an earth or other, feet south
eyes bleared west, waking to march.

General Fatigue stalked in, & a Major-General,
Captain Fatigue, and at the base of all
pale Corporal Fatigue,
and curious microbes came, came viruses:
and the Court conferred on Henry, and conferred on Henry
the rare Order of Weak.

—How come dims *one* these wholesome elsers oh?
Old polymaths, old trackers, far from home,
say how thro' auburn hair    titbits of youth's grey climb.
I have heard of rose-cheekt but the rose is here!
I bell:  when pops her phiz in    a good crow.
My beauty is off duty!—

Henry relives a lady, how down vain,
spruce in her succinct parts, spruce everywhere.
They fed like muscles and lunched
after, between, before. He tracks her, hunched
(propped on red table elbows) at her telephone,
white rear bare in the air.

Ill lay he long, upon this last return,
unvisited. The doctors put everything in the hospital
into reluctant Henry
and the nurses took it out & put it back,
smiling like fiends, with their eternal 'we.'
Henry did a slow burn,

collapsing his dialogue to their white ears
& shiny on the flanges. Sanka he drank
until his memories blurred
& Valerie was coming, lower he sank
and lovely. Teddy on his handlebars
perched, her. One word he heard

insistent: 'on.' He railed a stale abuse
upon his broad shortcomings, then lay still.
That middle-sized wild man was ill.
A hospital is where it all has a use,
so is a makar. . So is substantial God,
tuning in from abroad.

The surly cop lookt out at me in sleep
insect-like. Guess, who was the insect.
I'd asked him in my robe
& hospital gown in the elevator politely
why someone saw so many police around,
and without speaking he looked.

A meathead, and of course he was armed, to creep
across my nervous system some time ago wrecked.
I saw the point of Loeb
at last, to give oneself over to crime wholly,
baffle, torment, roar laughter, or without sound
attend while he is cooked

until with trembling hands hoist I my true
& legal ax, to get at the brains. I never liked brains—
it's the texture & the thought—
but I will like them now, spooning at you,
my guardian, slowly, until at length the rains
lose heart and the sun flames out.

Under the table, no. That last was stunning,
that flagon had breasts. Some men grow down cursed.
Why drink so, two days running?
two months, O seasons, years, two decades running?
I answer (smiles) my question on the cuff:
Man, I been thirsty.

The brake is incomplete but white costumes
threaten his rum, his cointreau, gin-&-sherry,
his bourbon, bugs um all.
His go-out privilege led to odd red times,
since even or especially in hospital things get hairy.
He makes it back without falling.

He sleep up a short storm.
He wolf his meals, lamb-warm.

Their packs bump on their '-blades, tan canteens swing,
for them this day my dawn's old, Saturday's IT,
through town toward a Scout hike.
For him too, up since two, out for a sit
now in the emptiest freshest park, one sober fling
before correspondence & breakfast.

Henry of Donnybrook bred like a pig,
bred when he was brittle, bred when big,
how he's sweating to support them.
Which birthday of the brighter darker man,
the Goya of the Globe & Blackfriars, whom—
our full earth smiled on him

squeezing his old heart with a daughter loose
(hostages they áre)—the world's produced,
so far, alarms, alarms.
Fancy the chill & fatigue four hundred years
award a warm one. All we know is ears.
My slab lifts up its arms

in a solicitude entire, too late.
Of brutal revelry gap your mouth to state:
Front back & backside go bare!
Cats' blackness, booze, blows, grunts, grand groans.
Yo-bad yōm i-oowaled bo    v'ha'l lail awmer h're gawber!
—Now, now, poor Bones.

I met a junior—not so junior—and
a-many others, who knew 'him' or 'them'
long ago, slightly,
whom I know. It was the usual
cocktail party, only (my schedule being strict)
beforehand.

I worked. Well. Then they kept the kids away
with their own questions, over briefest coffee.
Then kids drove me to my city.
I think of the junior: once my advanced élève,
sweetnatured, slack a little, never perhaps to make,
in my opinion then, it.

In my opinion, after a decade, now.
He publishes. The place was second-rate
and is throwing up new buildings.
He'll be, with luck, there always. —Mr Bones,
stop that damn dismal. —Why can't we all the same
be? —Dr Bones, how?

# *Temples*

He does not live here but it *is* the god.
A priest tools in atop his motorbike,
You do not enter.
He does not enter.
Us the landscape circles hard abroad,
sunned, stone. Like calls, too low, to like.

One submachine-gun cleared the Durga Temple.

It is very dark here in this groping forth

        Gulp rhubarb for a guilty heart,
rhubarb for a free, if the world's sway
waives customs anywhere that far

Look on, without pure dismay.
Unable to account for itself.

The slave-girl folded her fan & turned on my air-conditioner.
The lemonade-machine made lemonade.
I made love, lolled,
my roundel lowered. I ache less. I purr.
—Mr Bones, you too advancer with your song,
muching of which are wrong.

How this woman came      by the courage, how she got
the courage, Henry bemused himself in a frantic hot
night of the eight of July,
where it came from, did once the Lord frown down
upon her ancient cradle thinking 'This one
will do before she die

for two and seventy years of chipped indignities
at least,' and with his thunder clapped a promise?
In that far away town
who lookt upon my mother with shame & rage
that any should endure such pilgrimage,
growled Henry sweating, grown

but not grown used to the goodness of this woman
in her great strength, in her hope superhuman,
no, no, not used at all.
I declare a mystery, he mumbled to himself,
of love, and took the bourbon from the shelf
and drank her a tall one, tall.

A shallow lake, with many waterbirds,
especially egrets: I was showing Mother around,
An extraordinary vivid dream
of Betty & Douglas, and Don—his mother's estate
was on the grounds of a lunatic asylum.
He showed me around.

A policeman trundled a siren up the walk.
It was 6:05 p.m., Don was late home.
I askt if he ever saw
the inmates—'No, they never leave their cells.'
Betty was downstairs, Don called down 'A drink'
while showering.

I can't go into the meaning of the dream
except to say a sense of total LOSS
afflicted me thereof:
an absolute disappearance of continuity & love
and children away at school, the weight of the cross,
and everything is what it seems.

The sunburnt terraces which swans make home
with water purling, Macchu Pichu died
like Delphi long ago—
a message to Justinian closing it out,
the thousand years' authority, although
tho' never found exactly *wrong*

political patterns did indeed emerge;
the Oracle was conservative, like Lippmann,
roared the winds on the height,
The Shining Ones behind the shrine, whose verge
saw the impious plunged, 6000 statues
above the Temple shone

plundered, centuries plundered, first the gold
then bronze & marble, then the plinths,
then the dead nerve—
root-canal-work, ugh. I—I still hold
for the saviour of teeth, & I embrace
only he threw me a vicious

I consider a song will be as humming-bird
swift, down-light, missile-metal-hard, & strange
as the world of anti-matter
where they are wondering: does time run backward—
which the poet thought was true; Scarlatti-supple;
but can Henry write it?

Wreckt, in deep danger, he shook once his head,
returning to meditation. And word had sped
all from the farthest West
that Henry was desired: can he get free
of the hanging menace, & this all, and go?
He doesn't think so.

Therefore he shakes and he will sing no more,
much less a song as fast as said, as light,
so deep, so flexing. He broods.
He *may*, rehearsing, here of his bad year
at the very end, in squalor, ill, outside.
—Happy New Year, Mr Bones.

Welcome, grinned Henry, welcome, fifty-one!
I never cared for fifty, when nothing got done.
The hospitals were fun
in certain ways, and an honour or so,
but on the whole fifty was a mess as though
heavy clubs from below

and from—God save the bloody mark—above
were loosed upon his skull & soles. O love,
what was you loafing of
that fifty put you off, out & away,
leaving the pounding, horrid sleep by day,
nights naught but fits. I pray

the opening decade contravene its promise
to be as bad as all the others. Is
there something Henry miss
in the jungle of the gods whom Henry's prayer to?
Empty temples—a decade of dark-blue
sins, son, worse than you.

# 105

As a kid I believed in democracy: I
'saw no alternative'—teaching at The Big Place I ah
put it in practice:
we'd time for one long novel: to a vote—
*Gone with the Wind* they voted: I crunched 'No'
and we sat down with *War & Peace*.

As a man I believed in democracy (nobody
ever learns *any*thing): only one lazy day
my assistant, called James Dow,
& I were chatting, in a failure of meeting of minds,
and I said curious 'What are your real politics?'
'Oh, I'm a monarchist.'

Finishing his dissertation, in Political Science.
I resign. The universal contempt for Mr Nixon,
whom never I liked but who
alert & gutsy served us years under a dope,
since dynasty K swarmed in. Let's have a King
maybe, before a few mindless votes.

## 28 *July*

Calmly, while sat up friendlies & made noise
delight fuller than he can ready sing
or studiously say,
on hearing that the year had swung to pause
and culminated in an abundant thing,
came his Lady's birthday.

Dogs fill daylight, doing each other ill:
my own in love was lugged so many blocks
we had to have a vet.
Comes unrepentant round the lustful mongrel
again today, glaring at her bandages & locks:
his bark has grit.

This screen-porch where my puppy suffers and
I swarm I hope with hurtless love is now
towards the close of day
the scene of a vision of friendlies who withstand
animal nature so far as to allow
grace awhile to stay.

Three 'coons come at his garbage. He be cross,
I figuring porcupine & took Sir poker
unbarring Mr door,
& then screen door. Ah, but the little 'coon,
hardly a foot (not counting tail) got in with
two more at the porch-edge

and they swirled, before some two swerve off
this side of crab tree, and my dear friend held
with the torch in his tiny eyes
two feet off, banded, but then he gave &
shot away too. They were all the same size,
maybe they were brothers,

it seems, and is, clear to me we are brothers.
I wish the rabbit & the 'coons could be friends,
I'm sorry about the poker
but I'm too busy now for nipping or quills
I've given up literature & taken down pills,
and that rabbit doesn't trust me

Sixteen below. Our cars like stranded hulls
litter all day our little Avenue.
It *was* 28 below.
No one goes anywhere. Fabulous calls
to duty clank. Icy dungeons, though,
have much to mention to you.

At Harvard & Yale must Pussy-cat be heard
in the dead of winter when we must be sad
and feel by the weather had.
Chrysanthemums crest, far away, in the Emperor's garden
and, whenever we are, we must beg always pardon
Pardon was the word.

Pardon was the only word, in ferocious cold
like Asiatic prisons, where we live
and strive and strive to forgive.
Melted my honey, summers ago. I told
her true & summer things. She leaned an ear
in my direction, here.

She mentioned 'worthless' & he took it in,
degraded Henry, at the ebb of love—
O at the end of love—
in undershorts, with visitors, whereof
we can say their childlessness is ending. Love
finally took over,

after their two adopted: she has a month to go
and Henry has (perhaps) many months to go
until another Spring
wakens another Henry, with far to go;
far to go, pal.
My pussy-willow ceased. The tiger-lily dreamed.

All we dream, uncertain, in Syracuse & here
& there: dread we our loves, whereas the *National Geographic*
is on its way somewhere.
We're not. We're on our way to the little fair
and the cops & the flicks & the single flick
who'll solve our intolerable problem.

It was the blue & plain ones. I forget all that.
My own clouds darkening hung.
Besides, it wasn't serious.
They took them in different rooms & fed them lies.
'She admitted you wanted to get rid of it.'
'He told us he told you to.'

The Force, with its rapists con-men murderers,
has been our Pride (trust Henry) eighty years;—
now Teddy was hard on.
Still the tradition persists, beat up, beat on,
take, take. Frame. Get set; cover up.
The Saturday confessions are really something.

Here was there less or nothing in question but horror.
She left his brother's son two minutes but—
as I say I forget that—
during the time he drowned. The laundry lived
and they lived, uncharged, and went their ways apart
with the blessing of the N.Y. Police Force.

I miss him. When I get back to camp
I'll dig him up. Well, he can prop & watch,
can't he, pink or blue,
and I will talk to him. I miss him. Slams,
grand or any, aren't for the tundra much.
One face-card will do.

It's marvellous how four sit down—beyond
my thought how many tables sometimes are
in forgotten clubs
across & down the world. Your fever conned
us, pal. Will it work out, my solitaire?
The blubber's safe in the tubs,

the dogs are still, & all's well . . . nine long times
I loosed & buried. Then I shot him dead.
I don't remember why.
The Captain of the supply ship, playing for dimes,
thinks I killed him. The black cards are red
and where's the others? I—

My framework is broken, I am coming to an end,
God send it soon. When I had most to say
my tongue clung to the roof
I mean of my mouth. It is my Lady's birthday
which must be honoured, and has been. God send
it soon.

I now must speak to my disciples, west
and east. I say to you, Do not delay
I say, expectation is vain.
I say again, It is my Lady's birthday
which must be honoured. Bring her to the test
at once.

I say again, It is my Lady's birthday
which must be honoured, for her high black hair
but not for that alone:
for every word she utters everywhere
shows her good soul, as true as a healed bone,—
being part of what I meant to say.

# 113

## or Amy Vladeck or Riva Freifeld

That isna Henry limping. That's a hobble
clapped on mere Henry by the most high GOD
for the freedom of Henry's soul.
—The body's foul, cried god, once, twice, & bound it—
For many years I hid it from him successfully—
I'm not clear how he found it

But now he has it—much good may it do him
in the vacant spi*ritual* of space—
only Russians & Americans
to as it were converse with—weel, one Frenchman
to liven up the airless with one nose
& opinions clever & grim.

God declared war on Valerie Trueblood,
against Miss Kaplan he had much to say
O much to say too.
My memory of his kindness comes like a flood
for which I flush with gratitude; yet away
he shouldna have put down Miss Trueblood.

Henry in trouble whirped out lonely whines.
When ich when was ever not in trouble?
But did he whip out whines
afore? And when check in wif ales & lifelines
anyone earlier O? —Some, now, Mr Bones,
many. —I am fleeing double:

Mr Past being no friends of mine,
all them around: Sir Future Dubious,
calamitous & grand:
I can no foothold here; wherefore I pines
for Dr Present, who won't thrive to us
hand over neither hand

from them blue depths nor choppering down skies
does Dr Present vault unto his task.
Henry is weft on his own.
Pluck Dr Present. Let his grievous wives
thrall lie to livey toads. May his chains bask.
lower him, Capt Owen, into the sun.

Her properties, like her of course & frisky & new:
a stale cake sold to kids, a 7-foot weed
inside in the Great Neck night,
a record ('great'), her work all over as u-
sual rejected. She odd in a bakery.
The owner stand beside her

and she have to sell to the brother & sister jumping
without say 'One week old.' Her indifference
to the fate of her manuscripts
(which flash) to a old hand is truly somefing.
I guess: she'll take the National Book Award
presently, with like flare & indifference.

A massive, unpremeditated, instantaneous
transfer of solicitude from the thing to the creature
Henry sometimes felt.
A state of chancy mind when facts stick out
frequent was his, while that this shrugging girl,
keen, do not quit, he knelt.

(Having so swiftly, and been by, let down.)

Through the forest, followed, Henry      made his silky way.
No chickadee was troubled, small moss smiled
on his swift passage.
But there were those ahead when at midday
they met in a clearing and lookt at each other awhile.
To kill was not the message.

He only could go with them—odds? 20 to one-and-a-half:
pointless. Besides, palaver with the High Chief
might advance THE CAUSE.
Undoubtedly down they sat and they did talk
and one did balk & stuck but one did stalk
a creation of new laws.

He smoked the pipe of peace—the scene? tepees,
wigwams, papooses, buffalo hides, a high fire—
with everyone,
even that abnormally scrubbed & powerful one,
shivering with power, held together with wires,
his worst enemy.

Disturbed, when Henry's love returned with a hubby,—
I see that, Henry, I don't put that down,—
he thought he had to think
or with a razor like a skating-rink
have more to say or more to them downtown
in the Christmas season, like a hobby.

Their letters will, released, shake the mapped world
at some point, in the *National Geographic*.
(Friend, that hurt.)
It's horrible how near she was my hurt
in the old days—now she's a lawyer twirled
halfway around her finger

and I am elated & vague for love of her
and she is chilly & lost for love of me
and we are for each other
that which needs which, corresponding to Henry's mother
but which can not have, like the lifting sea
over each other's fur.

# 1 1 8

He wondered: Do I love? all this applause,
young beauties sitting at my feet & all,
and all.
It tires me out, he pondered: I'm tempted to break laws
and love myself, or the stupid questions asked me
move me to homicide—

so many beauties, one on either side,
the wall's behind me, into which I crawl
out of my repeating voice—
the mike folds down, the foolish askers fall
over theirselves in an audience of ashes
and Henry returns to rejoice

in dark & still, and one sole beauty only
who never walked near Henry while the mob
was at him like a club:
she saw through things, she saw that he was lonely
and waited while he hid behind the wall
and all.

Fresh-shaven, past months & a picture in New York
of Beard Two, I did have Three took off. Well. .
Shadow & act, shadow & act,
Better get white or you' get whacked,
or keep so-called *black*
& raise new hell.

I've had enough of this dying.
You've done me a dozen goodnesses; get well.
Fight again for our own.
Henry felt baffled, in the middle of the thing.
He spent his whole time in Ireland on the Book of Kells,
the jackass, made of bone.

No tremor, no perspire: Heaven is here
now, in Minneapolis.
It's easier to vomit than it was,
beardless.
There's always the cruelty of scholarship.
I once was a slip.

Foes I sniff, when I have less to shout
or murmur. Pals alone enormous sounds
downward & up bring real.
Loss, deaths, terror. Over & out,
beloved: thanks for cabbage on my wounds:
I'll feed you how I feel:—

of avocado moist with lemon, yea
formaldehyde & rotting sardines O
in our appointed time
I would I could a touch more fully say
my consentless mind. The senses are below,
which in this air sublime

do I repudiate. But foes I sniff!
My nose in all directions! I be so brave
I creep into an Arctic cave
for the rectal temperature of the biggest bear,
hibernating—in my left hand sugar.
I totter to the lip of the cliff.

Grief is fatiguing. He is out of it,
the whole humiliating Human round,
out of this & that.
He made a-many hearts go pit-a-pat
who now need never mind his nostril-hair
nor a critical error laid bare.

He endured fifty years. He was Randall Jarrell
and wrote a-many books & he wrote well.
Peace to the bearded corpse.
His last book was his best. His wives loved him.
He saw in the forest something coming, grim,
but did not change his purpose.

Honest & cruel, peace now to his soul.
He never loved his body, being full of dents.
A wrinkled peace to this good man.
Henry is half in love with one of his students
and the sad process continues to the whole
as it swarmed & began.

He published his girl's bottom in staid pages
of an old weekly. Where will next his rages
ridiculous Henry land?
Tranquil & chaste, de-hammocked, he descended—
upon which note the fable should have ended—
towards the ground, and

while fable wound itself upon him thick
and coats upon his tongue formed, white, terrific:
he stretched out still.
Assembled bands to do obsequious music
at hopeless noon. He bayed before he obeyed,
doing at last their will.

This seemed perhaps one of the best of dogs
during his barking. Many thronged & lapped
at his delicious stone.
Cats to a distance kept—one of their own—
having in mind that down he lay & napped
in the realm of whiskers & fogs.

Dapples my floor the eastern sun, my house faces north,
I have nothing to say except that it dapples my floor
and it would dapple me
if I lay on that floor, as-well-forthwith
I have done, trying well to mount a thought
not carelessly

in times forgotten, except by the *New York Times*
which can't forget. There is always the morgue.
There are men in the morgue.
These men have access. Sleepless, in position,
they dream the past forever
Colossal in the dawn comes the second light

we do all die, in the floor, in the morgue
and we must die forever, c'est la mort
a heady brilliance
the ultimate gloire
post-mach, probably in underwear
as we met each other once.

Behold I bring you tidings of great joy—
especially now that the snow & gale are still—
for Henry is delivered.
Not only is he delivered from the gale
but he has a little one. He's out of jail
also. It is a boy.

Henry's pleasure in this unusual event
reminds me of the extra told at Hollywood & Vine
that TV cameras
were focussed on him personally then & there
and 'Just a few words . . . Is it what you meant?
Was there a genuine sign?'

Couvade was always Henry's favourite custom,
better than the bride biting off the penises, pal,
remember? All the brothers
marrying her in turn & dying mutilated
until the youngest put in instead a crowbar, pal,
and pulled out not only her teeth but also his brothers' dongs & no
  doubt others'.

Bards freezing, naked, up to the neck in water,
wholly in dark, time limited, different from
initiations now:
the class in writing, clothed & dry & light,
unlimited time, till *Poetry* takes some,
nobody reads them though,

no trumpets, no solemn instauration, no change;
no commissions, ladies high in soulful praise
(pal) none,
costumes as usual, turtleneck sweaters, loafers,
in & among the busy Many who brays
art is if anything fun.

I say the subject was given as of old,
prescribed the technical treatment, tests really tests
were set by the masters & graded.
I say the paralyzed fear lest one's not one
is back with us forever, worsts & bests
spring for the public, faded.

# A Thurn

Among them marble where the man may lie
lie chicftains grand in final phase, or pause,
'O rare Ben Jonson',
dictator too, & the thinky other Johnson,
dictator too, backhanders down of laws,
men of fears, weird & sly.

Not of these least is borne to rest.
If grandeur & mettle prompted his lone journey
neither oh crowded shelves
nor this slab I celebrates attest
his complex slow fame forever (more or less).
I imagine the Abbey

among their wonders will be glad of him
whom some are sorry for     his griefs across the world
grievously understated
and grateful for that bounty, for bright whims
of heavy mind across the tiresome world
which the tiresome world debated, complicated.

Again, his friend's death made the man sit still
and freeze inside—his daughter won first prize—
his wife scowled over at him—
It seemed to be Hallowe'en.
His friend's death had been adjudged suicide,
which dangles a trail

longer than Henry's chill, longer than his loss
and longer than the letter that he wrote
that day to the widow
to find out what the hell had happened thus.
All souls converge upon a hopeless mote
tonight, as though

the throngs of souls in hopeless pain rise up
to say they cannot care, to say they abide
whatever is to come.
My air is flung with souls which will not stop
and among them hangs a soul that has not died
and refuses to come home.

A hemorrhage of his left ear of Good Friday—
so help me Jesus—then made funny too
the other, further one.
There must have been a bit. Sheets scrubbed away
soon all but three nails. Doctors in this city O
will not (his wife cried) come.

Perhaps he's for it. If that Filipino doc
had diagnosed ah here in Washington
that ear-infection ha
he'd have been grounded, so in a hall for the ill
in Southern California, they opined.
The cabins at eight thou'

are pressurized, they swore, my love, bad for—
ten days ago—a dim & bloody ear,
or ears.
They say are sympathetic, ears, & hears
more than they should or
did.

Thin as a sheet his mother came to him
during the screaming evenings after he did it,
touched F. J.'s dead hand.
The parlour was dark, he was the first pall-bearer in,
he gave himself a dare & then did it,
the thing was quite unplanned,

riots for Henry the unstructured dead,
his older playmate fouled, reaching for him
and never will he be free
from the older boy who died by the cottonwood
& now is to be planted, wise & slim,
as part of Henry's history.

Christ waits. That boy was good beyond his years,
he served at Mass like Henry, he never did
one extreme thing wrong
but tender his cold hand, latent with Henry's fears
to Henry's shocking touch, whereat he fled
and woke screaming, young & strong.

## 1 3 0

When I saw my friend covered with blood, I thought
This is the end of the dream, now I'll wake up.
That was more years ago
than I care to reckon, and my friend is not
dying but adhering to an élite group
in California O.

Why did I never wake, when covered with blood
I saw my fearful friend, his nerves are bad
with the large strain of moving,
I see his motions, stretcht on his own rack,
our book is coming out in paperback,
Henry has not ceased loving

but wishes all that blood would flow away
leaving his friend crisp, ready for all
in the new world O.
I see him brace, and on that note I pray
the blood recede like an old folderol
and he spring up & go.

Come touch me baby in his waking dream
disordered Henry murmured. I'll read you Hegel
and that will hurt your mind
I can't remember when you were unkind
but I will clear that block, I'll set you on fire
along with our babies

to save them up the high & ruined stairs,
my growing daughters. I am insane, I think,
they say & act so.
But then they let me out, and I must save them,
High fires will help, at this time, in my affairs.
I am insane, I know

and many of my close friends were half-sane
I see the rorschach for the dead on its way
Prop them up!
Trade us a lesson, pour me down a sink
I swear I'll love her always, like a drink
Let pass from me this cup

# A Small Dream

It was only a small dream of the Golden World,
now you trot off to bed. I'll turn the machine off,
you've danced & trickt us enough.
Unintelligible whines & imprecations, hurled
from the second floor, fail to impress your mother
and I am the only other

and I say go to bed! We'll meet tomorrow,
acres of threats dissolve into a smile,
you'll be the *Little* Baby
again, while I pursue my path of sorrow
& bodies, bodies, to be carried a mile
& dropt. Maybe

if frozen slush will represent the soul
which is to represented in the hereafter
I ask for a decree
dooming my bitter enemies to laughter
advanced against them. If the dream was small
it was my dream also, Henry's.

# 133

As he grew famous—ah, but what is fame?—
he lost his old obsession with his name,
things seemed to matter less,
including the fame—a television team came
from another country to make a film of him
which did not him distress:

he enjoyed the hard work & he was good at that,
so they all said—the charming Englishmen
among the camera & the lights
mathematically wandered in his pub & livingroom
doing their duty, as too he did it,
but where are the delights

of long-for fame, unless fame makes him feel easy?
I am cold & weary, said Henry, fame makes me feel lazy,
yet I must do my best.
It doesn't matter, truly. It doesn't matter truly.
It seems to be solely a matter of continuing Henry
voicing & obsessed.

Sick at 6 & sick again at 9
was Henry's gloomy Monday morning oh.
Still he had to lecture.
They waited, his little children, for stricken Henry
to rise up yet once more again and come oh.
They figured he was a fixture,

nuts to their bolts, keys to their bloody locks.
One day the whole affair will fall apart
with a rustle of fire,
a wrestle of undoing, as of tossed clocks,
and somewhere not far off a broken heart
for hire.

He had smoked a pack of cigarettes by 10
& was ready to go. Peace to his ashes then,
poor Henry,
with all this gas & shit blowing through it
four times in 2 hours, his tail ached.
He arose, benign, & performed.

I heard said 'Cats that walk by their wild lone'
but Henry had need of friends. They disappeared
Shall I follow my dream?
Clothes disappeared in a backward sliding, zones
shot into view, pocked, exact & weird:
who is what he seem?

I will tell you now a story about Speck:
after other cuts, he put the knife in her eye,
one of the eight:
he was troubled, missionary: and Whitman
of the tower murdered his wife & mother
before (mercy-killings) he set out.

Not every shot went in. But most went in:
in just over an hour
with the tumor thudding in his brain
he killed 13, hit 33:
his empty father said he taught him to respect guns
(not persons).

While his wife earned the living, Rabbi Henry
studied the Torah, writing commentaries
more likely to be burnt than printed.
It was rumoured that they needed revision.
Smiling, kissing, he bent his head not with 'Please'
but with austere requests barely hinted,

like a dog with a bone he worried the Sacred Book
and often taught its fringes.
Imperishable enthusiasms.
I have only one request to make of the Lord,
that I may no longer have to earn my living as a rabbi
'Thou shalt not make unto thee any graven image'

The sage said 'I merit long life if only because
I have never left bread-crumbs lying on the ground.
We were tested yesterday & are sound,
Henry's lady & Henry.
It all centered in the end on the suicide
in which I am an expert, deep & wide.'

Many's the dawn sad Henry has seen in,
many's the sun has lit his slouch to sleep,
many's a song to sing or vigil keep
of thought if you're made that way.
An incantation comes in nines: 'tahn . . bray':
heroes' bodies, in circles, thin,

collapsing. I don't understand this dream,
said Henry to himself in slippers: why,
things are going to pieces.
The furious bonzes sacked vast the Khmer temple
and thought fled: into the jungle. It was that simple.
Long after, spread the treatises.

Learned & otherelse, upon the ruins.
How is it faith finds ever matters rough?
My honey must flow off in the great rains,
as all the parts thereto do thereto belong
ha, and we are pitched toward the last love,
the last dream, the last song.

# Combat Assignment

Henry, moot, grunted. Like a lily of the valley
he dangled in the breeze of dreadful thought.
Look for the worst!
We came toward the world, did we not, accursed,
as witness crimes, but some craved out of that
like a Calcutta alley.

Grope for the cause. That won't be far away.
The Secretary of the Interior
may dog it from his grasp, or
we are divided together for the day
and all the some who have to say to me
are comfortably established, see?

There happened to occur a roar in the suctions
which rolled off the atmosphere, so we all gasped.
We do not know.
Perhaps it's as well the atmosphere rolled away:
think Dutch of the problems that would solve
including ours.

On which have sat so many distinguished friends,
old leather chair, take rest.
Your guts are showing.

# 139

Green grieves the Prince over his girl forgone
In the mists of the Hebrew & the Irish past
in the mists of the American past
I see him visit her, riding past at dawn
to watch her silver hair in a turret high
why did he leave her?

Grumbled to himself upon this ground the Rabbi
months. The knowing Books opened themselves in vain.
My Lord of Essex knew.
Some quirk of baffled pride led to a death due,
old men fail to follow either the pain—
why did he leave her?—

or the fascinated blood that led to an end:
cold as a toad lay suddenly half their love
and rode he by no more.
Celtic Henry groaned with his shoulder to the door
which never will close again, nor open enough—
why did he leave her?

Henry is vanishing. In the first of dawn
he fails a little, which he figured on.
Henry broods & recedes.
Like the great Walt, come find him on his way
somewhere. I hear thunder in stillness. She was a good lay.
Terror on Henry feeds

beginning with his knees. I saw his point,
remains much, probably, but not enough.
When the going got rough
elsewhere in the world lay Helen asleep with her secrets,
the poor man is coming to pieces joint by joint.
Does it advantage him, weak

with violent effort, rickety, on the stairs
It's a race with Time & that is all it is,
almost, given the conditions
& the faceless monsters of the Soviet Unions
The shadows, under the tower, in the most brilliant sun
will get us nowhere too.

# 1 4 1

One was down on the Mass. One on the masses.
Both grew Henry. What cause shall he cry
down the dead of Minnesota winter
without a singular follower nearby
among who seem to live entirely on passes
espouse for him or his printer?

Who gains his housing, heat, food, alcohol
himself & for his spouse & brood, barely.
Nude he danced in his snow
waking perspiring. He'd've run off to sea
(but for his studies careful of the Fall)
twenty-odd years ago.

Duly he does his needful little then
with a chest of ice, a head tipping with pain.
That perhaps is his programme,
cause: Henry for Henry in his main:
he'll push it: down with anything Bostonian:
even god howled 'I am'.

The animal moment, when    he sorted out her tail
in a rump session with the vivid hostess
whose guests had finally gone,
was stronger, though so limited, though failed
all normal impulse before her interdiction, yes,
and Henry gave in.

I'd like to have your baby, but, she moaned,
I'm married. Henry muttered to himself
So am I and was glad
to keep chaste. If this lady he had had
scarcely could he have have ever forgiven himself
and how would he have atoned?

—Mr Bones, you strong on moral these days, hey?
It's good to be faithful but it ain't natural,
as you knows.
—I knew what I knew when I knew when I was astray,
all those bright painful years, forgiving all
but when Henry & his wives came to blows.

—That's enough of that, Mr Bones. *Some* lady you make.
Honour the burnt cork, be a vaudeville man,
I'll sing you now a song
the like of which may bring your heart to break:
he's gone! and we don't know where. When he began
taking the pistol out & along,

you was just a little; but gross fears
accompanied us along the beaches, pal.
My mother was scared almost to death.
He was going to swim out, with me, forevers,
and a swimmer strong he was in the phosphorescent   Gulf,
but he decided on lead.

That mad drive wiped out my childhood. I put him down
while all the same on forty years I love him
stashed in Oklahoma
besides his brother Will. Bite the nerve of the town
for anyone so desperate. I repeat: I love him
until *I* fall into coma.

My orderly tender having too a gentle face
wants to be a Trappist but not to pray:
this convert lost his faith.
And douroucoulis out from their nesting place
peer with giant eyes, like lost souls, say:
but the whole fault ends with death.

Henry was almost clear on this subject, dying
as all we all are dying: death grew tall
up Henry as a child:
the truths that are revealed he is not buying:
he feels his death tugging within him, wild
to slide loose & to fall:

like the iron pear which rammed into his mouth
swells up to four times ordinary size
slowly cracking his skull open:
like the figure in a forest encountered, uncouth:
the oxygen tent: the consolation prize:
like the green pears which ripen.

Sorrow follows an evil     thought, for the time being only.

Also I love him: me he's done no wrong
for going on forty years—forgiveness time—
I touch now his despair,
he felt as bad as Whitman on his tower
but he did not swim out with me or my brother
as he threatened—

a powerful swimmer, to    take one of us along
as company in the defeat sublime,
freezing my helpless mother:
he only, very early in the morning,
rose with his gun and went outdoors by my window
and did what was needed.

I cannot read that wretched mind, so strong
& so undone. I've always tried. I—I'm
trying to forgive
whose frantic passage, when he could not live
an instant longer, in the summer dawn
left Henry to live on.

# VI

These lovely motions of the air, the breeze,
tell me I'm not in hell, though round me the dead
lie in their limp postures
dramatizing the dreadful word *instead*
for lively Henry, fit for debaucheries
and bird-of-paradise vestures

only his heart is elsewhere, down with them
& down with Delmore specially, the new ghost
haunting Henry most:
though fierce the claims of others, coimedela crime
came the Hebrew spectre, on a note of woe
and Join me O.

'Down with them all!' Henry suddenly cried.
Their deaths were theirs. I wait on for my own,
I dare say it won't be long.
I have tried to be them, god knows I have tried,
but they are past it all, I have not done,
which brings me to the end of this song.

Henry's mind grew blacker the more he thought.
He looked onto the world like the act of an aged whore.
Delmore, Delmore.
He flung to pieces and they hit the floor.
Nothing was true but what Marcus Aurelius taught,
'All that is foul smell & blood in a bag.'

He lookt on the world like the leavings of a hag.
Almost his love died from him, any more.
His mother & William
were vivid in the same mail Delmore died.
The world is lunatic. This is the last ride.
Delmore, Delmore.

High in the summer branches the poet sang.
His throat ached, and he could sing no more.
All ears closed
across the heights where Delmore & Gertrude sprang
so long ago, in the goodness of which it was composed.
Delmore, Delmore!

# 148

## *Glimmerings*

His hours of thought grew longer, his study less,
the data (he decided) were abundantly his,
or if not, never.
He called on old codes or new apperceptions,
he fought off an anxiety attack as the Lord did nations,
with brutal commitments, not clever.

Almost he lost interest in the 14 books part-done
in favour of insights fresh, a laziness in the sun,
rapid sketchings,
a violent level on the drop of friendship,
'I am pickt up & sorted to a pip,'
sleepless, watching.

Gravediggers all busy, Jelly, look what you done done
there died of late a great cat, a real boss cat
fallen from his prime
I'm sorry for those coming, I'm sorry for everyone
At least my friend is     rid of that
for the present space-time.

This world is gradually becoming a place
where I do not care to be any more. Can Delmore die?
I don't suppose
in all them years a day went ever by
without a loving thought for him. Welladay.
In the brightness of his promise,

unstained, I saw him thro' the mist of the actual
blazing with insight, warm with gossip
thro' all our Harvard years
when both of us were just becoming known
I got him out of a police-station once, in Washington, the world is *tref*
and grief too astray for tears.

I imagine you have heard the terrible news,
that Delmore Schwartz is dead, miserably & alone,
in New York: he sang me a song
'I am the Brooklyn poet Delmore Schwartz
Harms & the child I sing, two parents' torts'
when he was young & gift-strong.

## 150

He had followers but they could not find him;
friends but they could not find him. He hid his gift
in the center of Manhattan,
without a girl, in cheap hotels,
so disturbed on the street friends avoided him
Where did he come by his lift

which all we must or we would rapidly die:
did he remember the more beautiful & fresh poems
of early manhood now?
or did his subtle & strict standards allow
them nothing, baffled? What then did self-love show
of the weaker later, somehow?

I'd bleed to say his lovely work improved
but it is not so. He painfully removed
himself from the ordinary contacts
and shook with resentment. What final thought
solaced his fall to the hotel carpet, if any,
& the *New York Times*'s facts?

Bitter & bleary over Delmore's dying:
his death stopped clocks, let no activity
mar our hurrah of mourning,
let's all be Jews bereft, for he was one
He died too soon, he liked 'An Ancient to Ancients'
His death clouded the grove

I need to hurry this out before I forget
which I will never      He fell on the floor
outside a cheap hotel-room
my tearducts are worn out, the ambulance came
and there on the way he died
He was 'smart & kind,'

a child's epitaph. He had no children,
nobody to stand by in the awful years
of the failure of his administration
He was tortured, beyond what man might be
Sick & heartbroken Henry sank to his knees
Delmore is dead. His good body lay unclaimed
three days.

I bid you then a raggeder farewell
than at any time my grief would have desired,
you take secrets with you,
sudden appearances, and worse to tell,
vanishings. You said 'My head's on fire'
meaning inspired O

meeting on the walk down to Warren House
so long ago we were almost anonymous
waiting for fame to descend
with a scarlet mantle & tell us who we were.
Young poets are ridiculous, and rare
like a man death-wounded on the mend.

There's a memorial today at N.Y.U.,
your last appearance, old heroic friend.
I hope the girls are pretty
and the remarks radish-crisp befitting you
to allay the horror of your lonely end,
appease, a little, sorrow & pity.

# 153

I'm cross with god who has wrecked this generation.
First he seized Ted, then Richard, Randall, and now Delmore.
In between he gorged on Sylvia Plath.
That was a first rate haul. He left alive
fools I could number like a kitchen knife
but Lowell he did not touch.

Somewhere the enterprise continues, not—
yellow the sun lies on the baby's blouse—
in Henry's staggered thought.
I suppose the word would be, we must submit.
*Later.*
I hang, and I will not be part of it.

A friend of Henry's contrasted God's career
with Mozart's, leaving Henry with nothing to say
but praise for a word so apt.
We suffer on, a day, a day, a day.
And never again can come, like a man slapped,
news like this

Flagrant his young male beauty, thick his mind
with lore and passionate, white his devotion
to Gertrude only,
but even that marriage fell on days were lonely
and ended, and the trouble with friends got into motion,
when Delmore undermined

his closest loves with merciless suspicion:
Dwight cheated him out of a house, Saul withheld money,
and then to cap it all,
Henry was not here in '57
during his troubles (Henry was in Asia),
accusations to appall

the Loyal forever, but the demands increast:
as I said to my house in Providence
at 8 a.m. in a Cambridge taxi,
which he had wait, later he telephoned
at midnight from New York, to bring my family
to New York, leaving my job.

All your bills will be paid, he added, tense.

I can't get him out of my mind, out of my mind,
Hé was out of his own mind for years,
in police stations & Bellevue.
He drove up to my house in Providence
ho ho at 8 a.m. in a Cambridge taxi
and told it to wait.

He walked my living-room, & did not want breakfast
or even coffee, or even even a drink.
He paced, I'd say Sit down,
it makes me nervous, for a moment he'd sit down,
then pace. After an hour or so *I* had a drink.
He took it back to Cambridge,

we never learnt why he came, or what he wanted.
His mission was obscure. His mission was real,
but obscure.
I remember his electrical insight as the young man,
his wit & passion, gift, the whole young man
alive with surplus love.

I give in. I must not leave     the scene of this same death
as most of me strains to.
There are all the problems to be sorted out,
the fate of the soul, what it was all about
during its being, and whether he was drunk
at 4 a.m. on the wrong floor too

fighting for air, tearing his sorry clothes
with his visions dying O and O I mourn
again this complex death
Almost my oldest friend should never have been born
to this terrible end, out of which what grows
but an unshaven, disheveled *corpse*?

The spirit & the joy, in memory
live of him on, the young will read his young verse
for as long as such things go:
why then do I despair, miserable Henry
who *knew* him all so long, for better & worse
and nearly would follow him below.

Ten Songs, one solid block of agony,
I wrote for him, and then I wrote no more.
His sad ghost must aspire
free of my love to its own post, that ghost,
among its fellows, Mozart's, Bach's, Delmore's
free of its careful body

high in the shades which line that avenue
where I will gladly walk, beloved of one,
and listen to the Buddha.
His work downhill, I don't conceal from you,
ran and ran out. The brain shook as if stunned,
I hope he's over that,

flame may his glory in that other place,
for he was fond of fame, devoted to it,
and every first-rate soul
has sacrifices which it puts in play,
I hope he's sitting with his peers: sit, sit,
& recover & be whole.

Being almost ready now to say Goodbye,
my thought limps after you. I ring you up,
I know you are going tomorrow,
with gashed in me with you, I am I
gored with your leaving, for the 18th stop,
this stop is congratulation & sorrow,

you'll pay high rent & whizz. Blessings on you
the almost only surviving Jewess & Jew
since Delmore's dreadful death
who had no child in bitter early age
to turn him like a story, page on page,
until it wearieth

and then the child must outgo on its own:
outgo! My parting farewell on your sons
who will not replace you yet:
you are both young & old, fresh & worn, torn
but loving as I was in San Francisco once
and now yóu have that bit.

Panic & shock, together. They are all going away.
Henry took down his black four-in-hand & his black bowtie
and put away all other ties.
It is a pleasant Sunday summer afternoon,
I have been sick five times. Can I go on?
I am a half-closed book.

Exalted figures passed before Henry's eyes,
passed & withdrew. Retaining his faculties
barely, his trajectory,
his heart still beating in his empty breast,
he hollow-hearted waved to them going by
& out of sight.

I feel a final chill. This is cold sweat
that will not leave me now. Maybe it's time
to throw in my own hand.
But there are secrets, secrets, I may yet—
hidden in history & theology, hidden in rhyme—
come on to understand.

Halfway to death, from his young years, he failed
to keep on assigning to the concept 'love'
the usual value.
The heat of the chase yielded to ease & paled
midday which once he could not have enough of,
affections old to new

much he preferred, with one or two exceptions
which made up the existential difference
O and on these he banked,
Amy & Valerie hotted up his mail
which otherwise was dignified & stale
requests, to which he cranked

answers due, mostly too late, with slippers on,
'Thanks for the honour implied' chiefly he began
& let the rest dictate
indifferently itself: 'BUT I decline'
etc. whereas he raged bright orange in a pine
if his young ladies were late.

Draw on your resources. Draw on your resources.
It's not clear if I can. In a French town
Autun
where the grand cathedral stands, Henry's mental gown
amazed the residents, and his mental forces
exceeded Verdun.

But he was not up to that ancient sculpture;
cold & uneasy witnessed he them scenes:
the figures put him down.
The figures figure what the lost soul means,
so long ago, in an acre of sepulture
insisting on the verb, not the noun.

I wanted so to go to the Windward Islands,
and I will never make it, stuck in this French
vaulting cathedral thought.
We've been here long, long, lowlands & highlands
but not as they have. Draw on your mere *mensch*
for the benefits we sought.

## Vietnam

Henry shuddered: a war which was no war,
the enemy was not our enemy
but theirs whoever they are
and the treaty-end that might conclude it more
unimaginable than *Alice*'s third volume-eee—
and somehow our policy bare

in eighteen costumes kept us unaware
that we were killing Asiatics, daily,
with the disgusting numbers given
on my front page, at which, my love, I stare.
Better would be a definite war with the dragon,
taught to hate us wholly.

Better than the Buddhists self-incinerated
a colossal strike: on military targets
near eighteen Chinese cities.
That would make them think: as we have stated,
an end to aggression will open up new markets
and other quarter-lies.

Stomach & arm, stomach & arm
Henry endured like a pain-farm.
Nine o'clock, ten.
He workt all day & then he workt all night
and nothing that he made would tot out right
again.

The lust-quest seems in this case to be over:
Henry except for Amy has no lover,
Amy in a distant city
which fierce might be regarded as a pity
only that Henry's now respectable,
a householder, child & all.

Today's Thanksgiving; that is, summing up
that which one bears more steadily than else
and the odd definite good.
I do this thrice a year; that is, I grope
a few sore hours among my actuals
for evidence of knighthood.

Three limbs, three seasons smashed; well, one to go.
Henry fell smiling through the air below
and through the air above,
the middle air as well did he not neglect
but carefully in all these airs was wrecked
which he got truly tired of.

His friends alas went all about their ways
intact. Couldn't William break at least a collar-bone?
O world so ill arranged!
Henry holds in addition pharmacies
for all his other ills, pills of his own
which frequently get changed

as his despairing doctors change their minds
about what must be best for wilful Henry.
There seems to firm no answer
save from the sexton in the place that blinds
& stones and does not hurt: Henry springs youthfully
in his six-by-two like a dancer.

An orange moon upon a placid sea
glistened for criminal Henry's fiery arm
fractured in the humerus:
no joke to Henry, nothing humorous
about his broken, he loved emptily
the rest of his body, warm

but not too warm, like this delinquent member.
His fingers wiggle, wiggle too his toes
like a sound person's.
He found himself okay, save for dispersings
of pain across his gross shaft, hard as blows
that in deep woods fell timber.

O prostrate body, busy with your break,
false tissue forming, striving to recover,
when will you make do like the moon
cold on a placid sea, with three limbs, take
the other for a cruise, like an elderly lover
not expecting much.

I have strained everything except my ears,
he marvelled to himself: and they're too dull—
owing to one childhood illness—
outward, for strain; inward, too smooth & fierce
for painful strain as back at the onset, yes
when Henry keen & viable

began to poke his head from Venus' foam
toward the grand shore, where all them ears would be
if any.
Thus his art started. Thus he ran from home
toward home, forsaking too withal his mother
in the almost unbearable smother.

He strained his eyes, his brain, his nervous system,
for a beginning; cracked an ankle & arm;
it cannot well be denied
that nearly all the rest of him came to harm
too . . . Only his ears sat with his theme
in the splices of his pride.

## 167

### Henry's Mail

His mail is brimming with Foundation reports
and with the late inaction of the Courts
in his case, and his insurance firms
are rich with info enigmatic and
stuff stranger still from his main Bank is here to hand,
the Washington Post is all about germs,

and he and she want this and that—Christ God,
it's growing hard to get up in the morning
particularly since our postal service—
I hear Togo's is better: Couldn't we prod
that Cabinet jerk say into resembling
London or Paris

almost a hundred years ago

or the town in Okie-land when I was young—
three and four deliveries a day!—
now gives me, toward noon, ONE.
And I dote on my mail: I need its bung:
and the postman may indeed follow the moon and the sun
but believe me he fellows not Henry.

## The Old Poor

and God has many other surprises, like
when the man you fear most in the world marries your mother
and chilling other,
men from far tribes armed in the dark, the dike-
hole, the sudden gash of an old friend's betrayal,
words out that leave one pale,

milk & honey in the old house, mouth gone bad,
the caress that felt for all the world like a blow,
screams of fear eyeless, wide-eyed loss,
hellish vaudeville turns, promises had
& promises forgotten here below,
the final wound of the Cross.

I have a story to tell you which is the worst
story to tell that ever once I heard.
What thickens my tongue?
and has me by the throat? I gasp accursed
even for the thought of uttering that word.
I pass to the next Song:

Books drugs razor whisky shirts
Henry lies ready for his Eastern tour,
swollen ankles, one hand,
air reservations, friends at the end of the hurts,
a winter mind resigned: literature
must spread, you understand,

there's also the dough, to help out Vietnam.
Ha ha, no neckties, because of the sling
or is the arm that well
for neckties? It's doing what must be done,
helping them kill each other; that's the thing;
and keeping up appearances till

one miracle of one recovered arm
occurs, when Henry, without thinking about it,
can scratch his baffled head
in public or alone with either. Warm
should everybody mouth a lawless tit
at say thirty-three instead.

—I can't read any more of this Rich Critical Prose,
he growled, broke wind, and scratched himself & left
that fragrant area.
When the mind dies it exudes rich critical prose,
especially about Henry, particularly in Spanish, and sends it to him
from Madrid, London, New York.

Now back on down, boys; don't expressed yourself,
begged for their own sake sympathetic Henry,
his spirit full with Mark Twain
and also his memory, lest they might strain
theirselves, to alter the best anecdote
that even he ever invented.

Let the mail demain contain no pro's or con's,
or photographs or prose or sharp translations.
Let one-armed Henry be.
A solitaire of English, free of dons
& journalists, keeping trying in one or two nations
to put his boat back to sea.

Go, ill-sped book, and whisper to her or
storm out the message for her only ear
that she is beautiful.
Mention sunsets, be not silent of her eyes
and mouth and other prospects, praise her size,
say her figure is full.

Say her small figure is heavenly & full,
so as stunned Henry yatters like a fool
& maketh little sense.
Say she is soft in speech, stately in walking,
modest at gatherings, and in every thing
declare her excellence.

Forget not, when the rest is wholly done
and all her splendours opened one by one
to add that she likes Henry,
for reasons unknown, and fate has bound them fast
one to another in linkages that last
and that are fair to see.

Your face broods from my table, Suicide.
Your force came on like a torrent toward the end
of agony and wrath.
You were christened in the beginning Sylvia Plath
and changed that name for Mrs Hughes and bred
and went on round the bend

till the oven seemed the proper place for you.
I brood upon your face, the geography of grief,
hooded, till I allow
again your resignation from us now
though the screams of orphaned children fix me anew.
Your torment here was brief,

long falls your exit all repeatingly,
a poor exemplum, one more suicide
to stack upon the others
till stricken Henry with his sisters & brothers
suddenly gone pauses to wonder why he
alone breasts the wronging tide.

# In Mem: R. P. Blackmur

Somebody once pronounced upon one Path.
What rhythm shall we use for Richard's death,
the dearer of the dear,
my older friend of three blackt out on me
I am heartbroken—open-heart surgery—see!
but I am not full of fear.

Richard is quiet who talked on so well:
I fill with fear: I agree: all this is hell
Where will he lie?
In a tantrum of horror & blocking where will he be?
With Helen, whom he softened—see! see! see!
But not nearby.

Which search for Richard will not soon be done.
I blow on the live coal. I would be one,
another one.
Surely the galaxy will scratch my itch
Augustinian, like the night-wind witch
and I will love that touch.

# *Kyrie Eleison*

Complex his task: he threads the mazers daily,
sorts out from monsters saints *and* rewards them,
produces snow.
Blind his assistants, some in the Old Bailey,
some at the Waldorf Towers, the Pump Room,
trying their best O.

And he shall turn the heart of the children to their fathers
and this will not be easy. The wound talks to you.
It's light as a promise
to Rahab the spies'. Words light as feathers
fly. Wake with rage ruined limbs. Hoarfrost is blue
at dawn on the storm-windows.

Thuds. Almost floors. In the garden I am alone
among the animals. There is a shrill music
of which the less said the better.
Cold dough: is not that the one thing that might matter?
That, and the frightful fact that I am alone
while he sorts out the bloody saints.

Old King Cole was a merry old soul and a merry old soul was Henry
He called for his butts & he called for his bowl
& he called for his fiddlers three
in vain. Blank prose took hold of Henry's soul
considering all the deaths & considering.
There is a little life upstairs

playing her nursery rhymes to be considered
also. And there is a tall life out in the car
to be considered.
And there is the life of Henry's characters
to be thought on, established from afar.
Henry has much to do.

Take a deep breath then, sigh, relax, continue.
This world is a solemn place, with room for tennis.
Everybody's mouth
is somewhere else, I know, somebody's anus.
I speak a mystery, only to you.
Here's all my blood in pawn.

All that hair flashing over the Atlantic,
Henry's girl's gone. She'll find Paris a sweet place
as many times he did.
She's there now, having left yesterday. I held
her cousin's hand, all innocence, on the climb to the tower.
Her cousin is if possible more beautiful than she is.

All over the world grades are being turned in,
and isn't that a truly gloomy thought.
All over the world.
It's June, God help us, when the sight we fought
clears. One day when I take my sock
off the skin will come with it

and I'll run blood, horrible on the floor
the streaming blood reminds me of my love
Wolves run in & out
take wolves, but terrible enough
I am dreaming of my love's hair & all her front teeth are false
as were my anti-hopes.

Am tame now. You may touch me, who had thrilled
(before) your tips, twitcht from your breast your heart,
& burnt your willing brain.
I am tame now. Undead, I was not killed
by Henry's viewers but maimed. It is my art
to buzz the spotlight in vain,

flighting 'at random' while Addison wins.
I would not war with Addison. I love him
and Addison so loves me back
me backsides, I may perish in his grins
& grip. I would he liked me less, less grim.
But he has helpt me, slack

& sick & hopeful, anew to know what man—
scrubbing the multiverse with dazzled thought—
still has in store for man:
a doghouse or a cave, is all we could,
according to my dreams. I stand in doubt,
surrounded by holy wood.

Above the lindens tops of poplars waved
in an old French story, according to Henry
who shook himself & shaved,
rid of that dream. Rid slowly of all his dreams
he faced the wicked ordinary day
in a tumult of seems

whilst wanderers on coasts lookt for the man
actual, having encountered all his ghosts
off & on, by the way.
Murders occur in rain. Work while you can,
his hopeless spirit thrived to him to say
along those treacherous coasts.

*We are struck down*, repeat the chroniclers,
*having glowed*. Henry from hearsay
can vouch for most of this.
Leaving the known world with an awkward kiss
he haunted, back among     his colleagues in this verse
constructed in angry play.

A terrible applause pulls Henry's ear,
before the stampede: seats on seats collapse,
they are goring each other,
I donno if we'll get away. Who care?
Why don't we fold us down in our own laps,
long-no-see colleague & brother?

—I don't think's time to, time to, Bones.
Tomorrow be more shows; be special need
for rest & rehearse now.
Let's wander on the sands, with knitting bones,
while the small waves please the poor seaweed
so little. —The grand plough

distorts the Western Sky. Back to lurk!
We cannot rave ourselves. Let's hide. It's well
or ill,—there's a bell—so far,
the history of the Species: work, work, work.
All right, I'll stay. The hell with the true knell,
we'll meander as far as the bar.

# The Translator—I

(*Scene: Leningrad, the trials of the young poet Joseph
Brodsky for 'parasitism.' The judge's name deserves
record: one Mme Saveleva. Let her be remembered.*)

Henry rushes not in here. The matter's their matter,
and Hart Crane drowned himself some over money,
but it is Henry's mutter
that seldom has a judge so coarse borne herself coarsely
and often has a poet worked so hard for so small
but they was not prosecuted

in this world. It's Henry's matter, after all,
who is ashamed of much of the Soviet world
in their odium of imagination.
Translated not just Pole but Serbian
(a tough one, pal—vreme, vatre, vrtovi)
& Cuban: O a bevy!

They flocked to him like women, languages.
Bees honey but wound—African worst—Pasternak bees,
whom they not dared to touch
though after they ruin his friend, like this young man
who only wanted to walk beside the canals
talking about poetry and make it.

# The Translator—II

Because I am not able to forget,
Henry is dreaming of society,
one where the gifted & hard-working
young poet is cherished, kissed as a king
to come, a prized comer. Ah but see
them baleful ignorant

justicer & witnesses, corrupt by purity,
lacking all sense of others, lacking sense,
but liars too, pal.
I snuff the proper vomit of a State
where every tree is adjudged equal tall,
in faith without debate.

I beg to place in evidence, vicious mother:
That in the west of my land tower Douglas firs,
taller than others.
If then a judge grides to one of them 'You are sick,
lazy: Siberia!' what gross metaphors
shall we invent for this judge?

(The sentence: forced labour for five years in a 'distant locality.')

Buoyant, chockful of stories, Henry lingered
at party after party, a bitter-ender.
Long when the rest were asleep
he had much to relate, more to debate
if anyone would keep him company
toward fragrant dawn.

The river of his wide mind broke the jam,
somebody called his wild wit riverine,
sprayed thought like surf
assigned to angles none, curve upon curve,
such he *could* praise himself— —Mr Bones, you am.
Let's have a ritornello.

—Let's have a ritornello. You, me, her.
I loves you both and therefore all are bitter.
Let's have a ritornello.
He loved them many & he loved them well
and he held the world up like a big sea-shell
or heather-ale, harkening to follow.

## *News of God*

Eastward he longs, before, well, any bad
the silly fellow did. Then he remembers,
oh, the worst thing of all.
But he only remembers it as having been had,
not as itself—like a list of summers
surging into Fall.

High on which list lay one when Love licked him,
her own ice-cream cone, melting. Honey love:
again.
Swung hard a blind, hairy heavy grim
& unrememberable, over enough
of all that had been. Then

they were forever together. Her lip pearled,
sprang wet his front, for fear, the winning Prince,
who called back something . . . a plea?
Passing out of pity into the New World,
I ⌐mounted up. I sum it at five scents.
Bid for me.

Failed as a makar, nailed as scholar, failed
as a father & a man, hailed for a lover,
Henry slumped down, pored it over.
We c-can't win here, he stammered to himself.
With his friend Phil and also his friend Ralph
he mourned across or he wailed.

His friend Boyd waited, all behind the nurses,
the simple nurses pretty as you will,
and emerged, and gave.
*He* was as ill as well one can be, ill.
When he could read he studied for gravestones
the *Geographic,* with curses.

And neither did his friend Boyd haul him up
entirely, nor did Ralph & Phil succeed
dispersing his gross fears.
He leaned on Heaven; no. Black would he bleed
to tests. Their EEG for months, for years,
went mad. So did not he.

The drill was after or is into him.
Whirr went a bite. He should not feel this bad.
A truly first-class drill.
Nothing distinctly hurts. It reminds him.
—Like it makes you blink, Mr Bones, of was & will?
—Very much so.

Conundrums at the gum-line.
I've been jumpy for the last 37 years,
pal.
The more I lessen to, the bore I hears.
Drugging & prodding me! 'His Majesty,
the body.'

'Gynecomastia' the surgeon called,
'the man is old & bald
and has habits. In this circumstance
I cannot save him.' The older you get, at once
the better death looks and
the more fearful & intolerable.

There is a swivelly grace that's up from grace
I both remember & know. Into your face
for summers now—for three—
I have been looking, and for winters O
and never at any time have you resembled snow.
And at the ceremony

after His Honor swivelled us a judge
my best friend stood in tears, at both his age
and undeclining mine.
In E(e)rie Plaza then we kept on house
and months O soon we saw that pointy-nose
was destined to combine

her blood with Henry's in a little thing.
If all went well. It all went better, mingling,
and Little sprang out.
The parking-lot tilted & made a dance,
ditching Jesuits. The sun gave it a glance
and went about & about.

Them lady poets must not marry, pal.
Miss Dickinson—fancy in Amherst bedding hér.
Fancy a lark with Sappho,
a tumble in the bushes with Miss Moore,
a spoon with Emily, while Charlotte glare.
Miss Bishop's too noble-O.

That was the lot. And two of them are here
as yet, and—and: Sylvia Plath is not.
She—she her credentials
has handed in, leaving alone two tots
and widower to what he makes of it—
surviving guy, &

when Tolstoy's pathetic widow doing her whung
(after them decades of marriage) & kids, she decided he was *queer*
& loving his agent.
Wherefore he rush off, leaving two journals, & die.
It is a true error to marry with poets
or to be by them.

There is a kind of undetermined hair,
half-tan, to which he was entirely unable to fail to respond
in woman, a poisoned
reminiscence: a kiss, or so; there.
The lady is not pretty but has eyes,
and seems to be kind.

Convulsed with love, who cares? There is that hair
unbuttoned. Loves unbutton loves, we're bare,
somewhere in my mind.
When this occurs I begin to think in Spanish
when Miss Cienfuegos, who looked after me
& after me in Pasadena.

Murdered the ruses that would quack me clear
The orchard squeaks. I look less weird
without my beard
Cal has always manifested a most surprising affection
for Matthew Arnold,—who is not a rat but whom
I can quite take or leave.

The soft small snow gangs over my heavy house.
My ladies are well gone—but gone where? to Iowa!
the worst of them many states.
Bless the state of man of the man in Iowa.
One lady's left, the dog. She & I for days
have here to hang out.

My lady tucked our Twissy on a train,
stepped up herself, and they were off, for friends.
Their taxi wobbled away.
Our car won't start. It's twelve below. It won't rain
is the sole good news. Maybe in Ioway
it's worse. They'll get the 'bends'

as ladies & gentlemen do coming from Iowa,
pal. The gross snow hoods on the useless car.
We can't & must have that,
Bhuvaneswar Dog & I, spared Iowa.
The almost empty house in a tit for tat
is becoming a genuine bat.

The doomed young envy the old, the doomed old the dead young.
It is hard & hard to get these matters straight.
Keats glares at Yeats
who full of honours died & being old sung
his strongest. Henry appreciated that hate,
but what now of Yeats'

lucky of-Fanny-free feeling for Keats
who doomed by Mistress Gonne proved barren years
and saw his friends all leave,
stale his rewards turn, & cut off then at his peak,
promising in his seventies! all fears
save that one failed to deceive.

I scrounge ensamples violent by choice.
In most what matters, Henry wondered. Let's lie.
All we fall down & die
after a course worse of a stoppage of voice
so terrible I have no more to say
but best is the short day.

The autumn breeze was light & bright. A small bird
flew in the back door and the beagle got it
(half-beagle) on the second try.
My wife kills flies & feeds them to the dog,
five last night, plus one Rufus snapped herself.
This is a house of death

and one of Henry's oldest friends was killed,
it came on a friend' radio, this week,
whereat Henry wept.
All those deaths keep Henry pale & ill
and unable to sail through the autumn world & weak,
a disadvantage of surviving.

The leaves fall, lives fall, every little while
you can count with stirring love on a new loss
& an emptier place.
The style is black jade at all seasons, the style
is burning leaves and a shelving of moss
over each planted face.

Love me love me love me love me love me
I am in need thereof, I mean of love,
I married her.
That was a hasty & a violent step
like an unhopeful Kierkegardian leap,
wasn't it, dear?

Slowly the sloth moved on in search of prey,
I see that. The jungles flash with light,
in some angles dark as midnight,
and chuck chuck chuck the spark did make a noise
when he cross the street on de electric wires
but that sloth was all right.

Swiftly the wind rose, gorgons showed their teeth,
while the bombs bombed on empty territory beneath.
I love you.
Will I forget ever my sole guru
far in Calcutta. I do not think so.
Nor will I you.

Henry's friend's throat hurt. (Yvor Winters' dead.)
Reason & Nature cried out 'Operate!'
Of his high office
little he made with the trouble between his head
& chest. (Winters' last words marshalled with hate.)
Peculiar bliss

comes in relax. Decisions medics faced
(He thought the world of the East Coast: enemy.)
the Mayor faced no more,
relying in their hands, on memory based
& unforeseen conditions. (Henry set high
that Winters, his own sore

foe, like his cancer.) Now these two good men
wise in their years, ill in their bodies, lay
one gone, one to arrive
fixed, for our little time, & get up again:
Hurrah! (Alas.) Praising their—we may—
criteria & overdrive.

194

If all must hurt at once, let yet more hurt now,
so I'll be ready, Dr God. Púsh on me.
Give it to Henry harder.
There lives content: one area, taking a bow,
unbothered, whére I can't remember, lovely,
somewhere down there,

or, better still, up here, where forest fires
burn on for years. From the fire-towers watch is kept
on diminuendo flaming.
Each jack be the custodian of his desires
from which he sprang & sullen then he slept
until a coda of blaming.

—You do. She do. I will be with you-all,
in a little little silence, Mr Bones.
—I see I depend on you
for nothing. —Try Dr God, clown a ball,
low come to you in the blue sad darkies' moans
worsing than yours, too.

213

I stalk my mirror down this corridor
my pieces litter. Oklahoma, sore
from my great loss leaves me.
We pool our knowless in my seminar,
question all comers that they may not jar
their intrepidity

before the Awenger rises in the corpse's way
as inconvenient as the bloodscoot sway
of them Aztecs' real priests.
All my pieces kneel and we all scream:
History's Two-legs was a heartless dream,
reality is

& reskinned knuckles & forgiveness & toys
unbreakable & thunder that excites & annoys
but's powerless to harm.
Reality's the growing again of the right arm
(which so we missed in our misleading days)
& the popping back in of eyes.

I see now all these deaths are to one end—
whereby I lost a foe, friend upon friend—
room.
We wonder guided: it comes to all the same,
we too'll perform our rapture as of whom
later my love in whose name.

Fresh spring them enemies, decent fall the cloths
over a high income.
Vanish me later: here I'll stay while some
first put their glasses on the windowsill:
headlines the next day screamed until
even at Harvard the story was moths.

Harvard is after Henry, and that's not new.
'I'll see you later' cried the crippled soul
one destination behind.
Soul upon soul, in the high Andes, blue
but blind for turns. And this is where the mind
stops. Death is a box.

(I saw in my dream
the great lost cities, Macchu Picchu, Cambridge Mass., Angkor
I wonder if it's raining on Macchu Picchu or
Cambridge Mass, as here,
the terraces alive with magical rain
the dead all in their places, all insane
& trying to sit up from fear,

I saw it all, the peopled terraces
as once I suppose they were, as we are,
the peopled terraces,
slaves winding in & out, paying no income tax,
mostly brutal one to another,
I saw it all.

Baseball, & the utter    bloody fucking news,
converged on miserable Henry, eh?
Brother, they did.
Then how did Henry make itself of use?
apart, I mean, from these nuclear devices H & A.
Henry hid.

—I held all solid, then I let some jangle,
offended Henry whistled to itself.
How few followed
the One or both. Only some captains swallowed,
wondering. Many sprang in to untangle
the riddles of my little wit.

How tiresome Spenser's knights, their grave wounds overnight
annealed, whilst Henry with one broken arm
deep in hospital lay
with real pain between shots from light to light
ten lights, two specialists, where nurses swarm
day after achieveless day.

After all, it was solely the left arm
reminding me the whole body can come to harm;
will.
My wife puts off my sling: I cannot think:
I do my exercises. I wish all well,
including Mrs Randall Jarrell.

I dangle on the rungs, an open target.
The world grows more disgusting dawn by dawn.
There is a 'white backlash.'
When everything else fails on the auto, park it
& move away slowly. Obsolescent, on
the rungs, out of the car, 'ashes'.

Ashes, ashes, all fall down.
I will meet you then in the middle of the maidan
jump at monsoon dawn.
The bearer weeps, I'm going out so early.
How to account for me? I want her dearly
but being ill & so on

I stumble at the lift. Henry is dying.
Erect-squat in the corner, sweating, the bearer is crying.
I don't seem to make it down
Shall I finish on the landing? They *have* all waited
the foes fierce, others whom Henry baited,
a forest of bottles. —Mr Bones, you a clown.

## 200

I am interested & amazed: on the building across the way
from where I vaguely live there are no bars!
Best-looking place in town.
Only them lawyers big with great cigars
and lesser with briefcases, instead of minds,
move calmly in & out

and now or then an official limousine
with a live Supreme Court justice & chauffeur
mounts the ramp toward me.
We live *behind*, you see. It's Christmas, and *brrr*
in Washington. My wife's candle is out
for John F. Kennedy

and the law rushes like mud but the park is white
with a heavy fall for ofays & for dark,
let's exchange blue-black kisses
for the fate of the Man who was not born today,
clashing our tinsel, by the terrible tree
whereon he really hung, for you & me.

Hung by a thread more moments instant Henry's mind
super-subtle, which he knew blunt & empty & incurious
but when he compared it with his fellows'
finding it keen & full, he didn't know what to think
apart from typewriters & print & ink.
On the philosophical side

plus religious, he lay at a loss.
Mostly he knew the ones he would not follow
into their burning systems
or polar systems, Wittgenstein being boss,
Augustine general manager. A universal hollow
most of the other seems;

so Henry in twilight is on his own:
marrying, childing, slogging, shelling taxes,
pondering, making.
It's rained all day. His wife has been away
with genuine difficulty he fought madness
whose breast came close to breaking.

With shining strides hear his redeemer come,
in a hospital gown, bringing     to bear on some
more than they well can bear.
Huge & dark stairwells see the one draw down
with a strange expression, neither smile nor frown,
intense, through trembling air.

What can be piled on Henry Henry can take,
peine forte et dure, and never will his silence break.
Ex-nuns line
the circle of the room of recognition
transfixed in Schadenfreude like a mission.
The orderlies serve wine

while slow the ex-priest hauls a frantic breath
and the gong clangs, meaning this way is death.
We still have some to go
when a blessed sweating waking heaves between
this body lunging and the horrid scene
alive back there below.

Nothing! —These young men come to interview me
armed with taperecorders, cameras,
the best ways of getting at you
so far invented save the telephone
and it costs money now to be alone:
to shut it off you need two

I have two & they ring from dawn to eve,
with extras in the night—can't shut them down:
awaiting a long distance call.
I read the 'paper gingerly lest I grieve,
ignore the radio & TV, don't go downtown:
truly isolated, pal.

However, I shudder & the world shrugs in,
hilarious loves walking the streets like trees
minus an ear,
men from far tribes armed in the dark, women
cantering in from the plains just as they please
with the water up to here.

Henry, weak at keyboard music, leanèd on
the slow movement of Schubert's Sonata in A
& the mysterious final soundings
of Beethoven's 109–10–11 & the Diabelli Variations
You go by the rules but there the rules don't matter
is what I've been trying to say.

Huddled, from their recesses, the goblins spring
(I'm playing it as softly as I can)
while the sound goes roaring.
If I scream, who would hear me? Rilke, come on strong
& forget our rôles, we'll play the Housman man
unless, of course, all this is boring.

Tides bring the bodies back sometimes, & not.
The bodies of the self-drowned out there wait,
wait, & the widows wait,
my gramophone is the most powerful in the country,
I am trying, trying, to solve the andante
but the ghost is off before me.

Come & dance, Housman's hopeless heroine
bereft of all: I take you in me arms
burnt-cork:
your creator is studying his celestial sphere,
he never loved you, he never loved a woman
or a man, save one: he was a fork

saved by his double genius & certain emendations
All his long life, hopeless lads grew cold
He drew their death-masks
To listen to him, you'd think that growing old
at twenty-two was horrible, and the ordinary tasks
of people didn't exist.

He did his almost perfect best with what he had
Shades are sorrowing, as not called up
by in his genius him
Others are for his life-long omission glad
& published their works as soon as he came to a stop
& could not review them.

Come again closer, Dr Swift & Professor Housman,
you have in common—I repeat, in common—
a certain failure in youth:
which you ruined, with your hard-earn'd learning:
seven years it took you, ancient Dean,
& Housman came to truth

only after ledgering, endless ledgering
& then he squandered his brains on the youths at Cambridge—
my own university!—
he would accept no honours, he proud as Swift,
merely refused them. Swift, infinitely greater
but far more imperfect

I hear as chiding that distinguisht man
but the Dean must be careful: Housman lost his degree
because he would not take
the Platonic argument beyond what was necessary
to *establish the text*. Therefore he failed
& became the first scholar in Europe.

—How are you? —Fine, fine. (I have tears unshed.
There is here near the bottom of my chest
a loop of cold, on the right.
A thing hurts somewhere up left in my head.
I have a gang of old sins unconfessed.
I shovel out of sight

a-many ills else, I might mention too,
such as her leaving and my hopeless book.
No more of that, my friend.
It's good of you to ask and) How are you?
(Music comes painful as a happy look
to a system nearing an end

or an empty question slides to a standstill
while the drums increase inside an empty skull
and the whole matter breaks down
or would it would, had Henry left his will
but that went sideways sprawling, collapsed & dull.)
How are you, I say with a frown.

His mother wrote *good* news: somebody was still living.
His wife gave him a hard time, unforgiving.
He romped on the floor with his daughter.
A special number of the London TLS came
and he studied the Asiatic & European
brains of late, across the water,

and some of the articles were spectacularly stupid
but most were par—though there appeared no Cupid—
Vozhnezsensky was good on watermelons
and Nevada's Miss Breadlove outstripp~d the felons
to be crowned the Narrative Poet Laureate of North America.
Groovy, pal.

So many thinking & feeling, in so many languages
as it has probably, women barred, down the ages,
but seldom so frisky as now.
Risky & slavish looks the big big scene.
Henry his horns waved at the future of poetry, where he had been,
and hid back in his shell-ow.

Henry lay cold & golden in the snow
toward whom the universe once more howled 'No'—
once more & again.
'What pricks have you agin' me, —liquor laws,
the appearance in my house of owls & saws,—
decanted unto the world of men?'

'Divulge we further: somewhat is because
you loner, you storm off away without pause
across the sad ice
overlain with the tricky new of all the snow
whereat my Sisters up in Him sang 'So:
he's coming: 'twill be nice?'

Darker, of the beginning of their hopes,
the huddled end, toward which the lost cork gropes.
I seize the neck of the bottle
& smash it on my sink, when from both ends
it spurts, it rides, as if to blow amends
for the earlier part of the bottle.

—Mr Blackmur, what are the holy cities of America?
Sir Herbert's son, who lives near Canterbury,
precocious, asked my friend.
A brain can stammer: Henry's friend's did: 'Er . . . er . . .'
Pilgrimages to Palm Springs smother me,
I'm retreating to Atlantic City.

Atlantic City in the winter is worth having: holy it's not,
empty it is, and who knows anybody in Atlantic City?
His doctors drove him there
for privacy: at the biggest bar in the world,
down his hotel, shared now with a man a football field away,
he had one drink.

The Boardwalk, keen winds, & the timeless surf
& the medieval torture-instruments from Nuremberg
& shrunken heads for dollars
and home he fled, abroad he streamed, to Autun
& places else where holiness held forth
& then slunk back to his north.

# 211

Forgoing the Andes, the sea-bottom, Angkor,
he led with his typewriter. He made it fly
& walk to them sites for him.
He led with his tongue & taught & taught & taught,
forgoing Truro, to mollify one creditor
or another.

The heat made headlines, while he lectured on,
drencht.
Ouzo was peaceful in the fearful nights,
a gift from a Spartan lady
whose life has been so far    so much worse even than his
that he stifled an American scream.

Of the stately sights he had his modicum,
it's true: the Campidoglio, e.g.
But mostly, though, the grindstone & the nose
had it, & him, like Fragor
When nostalgia for things unknown grips him he growls
he's saving it for the next time around.

With relief to public action, briefly stopt
the lonely stalking of phrasing & concept:
I'll begin like a cannon
or canon: I think the elder statesman stance will do.
I will wear my bearded difference with rue
before the damned young things

flashy for knowledge of they dream not what
until I drop the Bacchae in its slot:
take that! and that!
Also his brains accumulates its fat
until their priest, squat on the altar, Skat,
reluctant as my tot.

The women scream adown the mountain side
& the frisky god screams, as full well he may,
worst is the armed mother:
night with her knives reigns. I will stay the night
and I have nothing more much now to say
in the brilliance of their smother.

Wan shone my sun on Easter Monday,—ay,
on Monday wan, and yet the snow has ceast.
Filthy, my grass appears.
Pavements appear. It's spring in Minnesota.
My summerhouse limps. My friends in the East
stalk robins, & dot their fears.

One of my steps is broken, free from ice,
I notice. Henry's steps sag in the blue
lost of Louisiana.
He was always in love with the wrong woman
we can't go on here, which would not be nice
nor true.

Horror absolved his movement's strange. He hangs on
Azured the star over the tower at the top of the hill,
the Mayor's wife sank into grateful sleep
by his good side
blonde, touseled, back from Washington.
In which pale sun we abide.

Jews being better than us others, still . . .

Which brandished goddess wide-eyed Henry's nights—
the temperature was even, the sky was still—
tell me, which one?
Was it the one with the curve to her left knee—
hidden her face with swung hair, masked her delights—
or was it another one?

Tribunals converged in vain. Honours swung to him
doing him less good. He had a court case
he was bound to lose.
Photographers & reporters swarmed, as of an honour
which all thought it was, whereupon he had
a Chinese nightmare, whose?

Back to the knee. We must not the divine knee
swiftly forget. Her family don't talk,
nobody lately talks.
My friends are ill or dead, who goes for walks?
In the atlas of Henry's women
your happy map would be a folding map.

# 215

Took Henry tea down at the Athenaeum with Yeats
and offered the master a fag, the which he took,
accepting too a light
to Henry's lasting honour. Time abates.
Humourless, grand, by the great fire for a look
he set out his death in twilight.

The goddamned scones came hot.

He coughed with his sphincter, when it hurt
Henry, who now that fierceness imitates.
Empires fall, arise semi-states,
Kleenex improves, clings to its own our dirt
the foul same. The last of the girls had gone
half in despair on.

He starved & flung him on 'em. Fat then, free,
he make a lukewarm wooer. All this hell of flesh—
not so bulk', after all—
keeps him from edge, as forever he will be—
how rottenly the prize collapse from fresh—
a taller man than, we thought, tall.

'Scads a good eats', dere own t'ree cars, the 'teens
(until of them shall be asked one thing, they romp or doze)
have got it made;
no prob. was ever set them, their poor ol' jerks
of parents *loved* them, with deep-freeze, & snacks
would keep a Hindu family-group alive.

Well, so they're liars & gluttons & cowards: so what?
. . . It's the Land of Plenty, maybe about to sigh.
Why shouldn't they terrify
with hegemony Dad (stupido Dad) and teach'?
(The tanks of the elders roll, in exercise, on the German plain.)
Even if their sense is to (swill &) die

why don't they join us, pal, as Texas did
(the oil-mailed arrogant butt), and learn how to speak
modestly, & with exactness, and
. . . like a sense of the country, man? Come off it. Powers,
the fêted traitor, became so in hours,
and the President, ignorant, didn't even lie.

Some remember ('Pretty well') the Korean war.
The unrecruited memory seems to embrace
the Bay of Pigs, Franklin Roosevelt. Who has in mind
with a shudder Cold Harbor,—
Henry is schlaft in his historical moode,—
with pity & horror the Bloody Angle?
Good Friday, and the end?

Three like terrifying political murders
have cast, as Adams sighed, no shadow on the Whites' House.
—Adhere, Sir Bones, to Heaven; tho' the shrine is still,
what here or there but by the will
of hidden God git done? Ah ask.
—I have an answer lost here on my desk:

Pakistan may Pakistan, well, find;
or not.
Henry couldn't care less.
—Mr Bones, cares for all men!
—Overloaded. It is my country     in my country only
cast is our lot.

Fortune gave him to know the flaming best,
expression's kings in his time, by voice & hand,—
the Irishman,
the doomed bard roaring down the thirsty west,
the subtle American British banker-man
and the lunatic one

fidgeting, with bananas, and his friend the sage
(touchy, 'I'm very touchy') in his cabin
two miles from mine here,
and already now let's call it a strong age,
not just a science age, as idiot habit
cries; I'm getting near

an end, but I add on the Bostonian,
rugged & grand & sorrowful. That's six,
and that's enough.
Henry as I was muttering knew them man
by man: much good it did him in his fix
except for letting out love.

## So Long? Stevens

He lifted up, among the actuaries,
a grandee crow. Ah ha & he crowed good.
That funny money-man.
Mutter we all must as well as we can.
He mutter spiffy. He make wonder Henry's
wits, though, with a odd

. . . something . . . something . . . not there in his flourishing art.
O veteran of death, you will not mind
a counter-mutter.
What was it missing, then, at the man's heart
so that he does not wound? It is our kind
to wound, as well as utter

a fact of happy world. That metaphysics
he hefted up until we could not breathe
the physics. *On our side*,
monotonous (or ever-fresh)—it sticks
in Henry's throat to judge—brilliant, he seethe;
better than us; less wide.

—If we're not Jews, how can messiah come?
Praise God, brothers, Who is a coloured man.
(Some time we'll do it again,
in whiteface.) 'Rám,' was his last word, like 'Mary'
or 'OM' or a perishing new grunt.
(winged 'em.) Kingdom? Some.

My God! they'm be surprised to see Your face,
all your admirers, in their taffeta,
or—upon thought—not all:
we will not wonder, will us, Mr Bones,
when either He looms down or wifout trace
we vanisheth. It's tall

time now in Ghetto-town: it's curtain-call:
hard now to read the time. Seem to Me I'm
not altogether the same
pro-man I strutted out from the wings as,
like losing faith. Counsel me, Mr Bones.
—my friend, the clingdom has come.

I poured myself out thro' my tips. What's left?
I slipt. I slipt. What's right? Whose centre's where?
His son has set.
Their towers lean & wobble. Anything I sang
I take back. Crimson is succeeded by black;
it is a fact.

Beckett shuddered, with thought. An unspeakable sound
of typing chittered to me in the night
as I sat thinking.
Pray as I would, dawn came to my hills:
in perfect silence I took out my laundry
and had *it* done.

If the blood banged, as it must do, faint
with necessity, forgive it, please. 'I paint'
(Renoir said) 'with my penis.'
A picture in Philadelphia proves it. Pal,
in wars & loves when we lost ground, how shall
we know who it means?

It *was* a difficult crime to re-enact,
Fatty's; if crime it were. Was he so made
as to be dangerous?
or if she'd gone to the john beforehand might
in the middle of his love she have been all right
or was there shoved ice?

This burning to sheathe it which so many males
so often and all over suffer: why?
Is it: to make or kill
is jungle-like what constitutes my I,
so let's thrust? When both crimes lead into wails,
at once or later. Tales

told of these truths stand up like goldenglow
head-high, and around the planet men are erect
and girls lie ready:
a bounce, toward pain. Melons, they say, though,
are best—I don't know if that's correct—
as well as infertile, it's said.

It's wonderful the way cats bound about,
it's wonderful how men are not found out
so far.
It's miserable how many      miserable are
over the spread world at this tick of time.
These mysteries that I'm

rehearsing in the dark did brighter minds
much bother through them ages, whom who finds
guilty for failure?
Up all we rose with dawn, springy for pride,
trying all morning. Dazzled, I subside
at noon, noon be my gaoler

and afternoon the deepening of the task
poor Henry set himself long since to ask:
Why? Who? When?
—I don know, Mr Bones. You asks too much
of such as you & me & we & such
fast cats, worse men.

# *Eighty*

Lonely in his great age, Henry's old friend
leaned on his burning cane while his old friend
was hymnéd out of living.
The Abbey rang with sound. Pound white as snow
bowed to them with his thoughts—it's hard to know them though
for the old man sang no word.

Dry, ripe with pain, busy with loss, let's guess.
Gone. Gone them wine-meetings, gone green grasses
of the picnics of rising youth.
Gone all, slowly. Stately, not as the tongue
worries the loose tooth, wits as strong as young,
only the albino body failing.

Where the smother clusters pinpoint insights clear.
The tennis is over. The last words are here?
What, in the world, will they be?
White is the hue of death & victory,
all the old generosities dismissed
while the white years insist.

# Pereant qui ante nos nostra dixerunt

Madness & booze, madness & booze.
Which'll can tell who preceded whose?
What chicken walked out on what egg?
*I* can tell, which am which oblong.
Corroborate, Los Alamos. —We read you. Wrong.
—I put up my radar & beg:

Corroborate from Berkeley. —Wrong. —Corrob
O from Woods Hole. —No wish to bob
your cred', but we knew that.
Yes. Confirmed, confirmed.
—Dance in my corridors, under the orange-grey moon,
stuff on your glory hat,

and potstill highland malt that whisky out
swifter than missles to the side of the hill,
the side of the sweet hill,
where installations live forever, about.
Up Scotland! who only drunky sexy Burns
producing, which returns.

Phantastic thunder shook the welkin, high.
The animals sat face to face & glared.
Henry was afraid.
Her love, which was not exactly that of a maid,
failed to assuage his terrible fears, who fared
forth in such a world.

Arose from throats anguish. Disappeared in air
many, and many on the ground, and many at sea.
It was not a place to love.
Thumbs into eyes, enormous explosions of
what we know not, until sobriety became a vice.
'Our breakdowns guarantee us,' said a pal.

I saw her in a dream, from my dream she woke,
pleasantness & courtesy & love
and all them stuff.
She had long hair as if long hair enough
to smother horrors. What with her in the smoke
he did he will not say.

Profoundly troubled over Miss Birnbaum—
a photograph! from Heaven! by Heaven, please!—
Henry rocked on knees
tortured with his project: Lebensraum!
(Unused to pray, he ache.) Away with treaties!
Lassen Sie uns

herausgehen! (Bony, either, his knees hurt,
all over he hurt.) Down with the superior race!
One look more at that face
live enchanting would      trance Henry to assert
ideologies weird: take her aways:
disband the Bunds:

leave wizard Henry: at his lectern where
he's working on his phantasies: Disperse!
and everything goes worse
so the world fills with hér knees, harmful & fair:
a medium where 'Fuck you' comes as no curse
but come as a sigh or a prayer.

The Father of the Mill surveyed his falls,
his daughterly race, his flume, his clover, privy, of all
his waterfall, found well.
Rain fell in June like . . . grace? One flopping trout
(a rainbow) make his lunch who took his bait.
Pitch, & Fate flout.

Each cat should seizing private waterfall,
or rent, as Henry do. Seizure is gall,
I guess. Yes;
we nothing own. But we are lying owned.
When last his burning publisher telephoned,
he dying to confess.

The father and the mill purveyed their falls:
grist, grist! Still, stamping on Fate,
he lauded his lady;
ladies. Waders were treble at his end
or ends. The fool danced in the waterfall
losing his footing, ready.

They laid their hands on Henry, kindly like,
and swooped him thro' the major & minor orders
and said to him: 'You're in business.'
'*OW*' he responded. It was raining at the time,
or cascading, or the seas were climbing up out of their borders,
when he took up Is-ness.

Dragons, good dragons, sport in the violent foam
on the second floor of the Boston Art Museum
in the joy of the dead Sung Master.
Tigers were friendly: they do not kill needless
and remove pests; dragons are male, yes.
The subject: triumph—disaster.

God's own problem, whistled the whiskey priest.
I cannot help him. But, if he repents,
I'll do what I can, man.
Like exorcize: a slow process: at least,
unless he dies, he'll scream with less vehemence
and we'll get the Devil a bus ticket.

There are voices, voices. Light's dying. Birds have quit.
He lied about me, months ago. His friendly wit
now slid to apology.
I am sorry that senior genius remembered it.
I am nothing, to occupy his thought
one moment. We

went at his bidding to his cabin, three,
in two bodies; and he spoke like Jove.
I sat there full of love,
salt with attention, while his jokes like nods
pierced for us our most strange history. He
seemed to be in charge of the odds:

hurrah. Three. Three. I must remember that.
I love great men I love. Nobody's great.
I must remember that.
We all fight. Having fought better than the rest,
he sings, & mutters & prophesies in the West
and is our flunked test.

I always come in prostrate; Yeats & Frost.

*Ode*

To That Boring Shit James Thomson, Seasonal

Now gently rail on Henry Pussycat,
for he *did bad,* and punisht he must be,
by them, & by *them,* & by all.
He'll lose his place (in the book) and each thing that
ever he valued. He'll lose his minstrelsy.
Vainly will topics call

for cunning putting to who smashed his lyre,
drowned his harmonica, covered with foes,
and coughed with horror, & gave uts.
One word of *them:* (he'll lose his scholar-ire,
*pereant qui . .)* a voyeur, O and those
the slob's associates

the aggressive tease shockfull of malice, the dead-end
out-of-conflict father, the clever brother & the dull,
the nosey Jesuit.
A tribe to lose to: *I* lose my right hand,
she lost the honour of her word, ah well
Henry fell among . . it.

They work not well on all but they did for him.
He wolfed friend breakfast, bolted lunch, & pigged
dinner.
Beastly yet, meat at midnight, juice he swigged,
juices, avocado lemon'd, artichoke hearts,
anything inner,

except the sauce. Stand Henry off the sauce.
He scrub himself, have nine    more matchless cigarettes,
waiting upon the Lord.
Pascal drop in, they placing cagey bets,
it's midnight! Being ample in their skins
they hang around bored.

Negroes, ignite! you have nothing to use but your brains,
which let bust out. —What was that again, Mr Bones?
De body have abuse
but is de one, too. —One-two, the old thrones
topple, dead sober. The decanter, pal!
Pascal, we free & loose.

## Cantatrice

Misunderstanding. Misunderstanding, misunderstanding.
Are we stationed here among another thing?
Sometimes I wonder.
After the lightning, this afternoon, came thunder:
the natural world makes sense: cats hate water
and love fish.

Fish, plankton, bats' radar, the sense of fish
who glide up the coast of South America
and head for Gibraltar.
How do they know it's there? We call this *instinct*
by which we dream we know what instinct is,
like misunderstanding.

I was soft on a green girl once and we smiled across
and married, childed. Never did we truly take in
one burning wing.
Henry flounders. What is the name of that fish?
So better organized than we are oh.
Sing to me that name, enchanter, sing!

# The Carpenter's Son

The child stood in the shed. The child went mad,
later, & saned the wisemen. People gathered
as he conjoined the Jordan joint
ánd he spoke with them until he got smothered
amongst their passion for      mysterious healing had.
They could not take his point:

—Repent, & love, he told them frightened throngs,
and it is so he did. Díd some of them?
Which now comes hard to say.
The date's in any event a matter of wrongs
later upon him, lest we would not know him,
medieval, on Christmas Day.

Pass me a cookie. O one absolutely did
lest we not know him. Fasten to your fire
the blessing of the living God.
It's far to seek if it will do as good
whether in our womanly or in our manlihood,
this great man sought his retire.

Tears Henry shed for poor old Hemingway
Hemingway in despair, Hemingway at the end,
the end of Hemingway,
tears in a diningroom in Indiana
and that was years ago, before his marriage say,
God to him no worse luck send.

Save us from shotguns & fathers' suicides.
It all depends on who you're the father *of*
if you want to kill yourself—
a bad example, murder of oneself,
the final death, in a paroxysm, of love
for which good mercy hides?

A girl at the door: 'A few coppers pray'
But to return, to return to Hemingway
that cruel & gifted man.
Mercy! my father; do not pull the trigger
or all my life I'll suffer from your anger
killing what you began.

When Henry swung, in that great open square,
the crowd was immense, the little clouds were white
and it was all well done.
It's true he did it, because more to bear
of her open eyes & mute mouth at midnight
behind her little counter

by the others mangled, trying on her throat
with a lard knife: he took his shoemaker's
and it was all well done.
For more to bear he could, ha he could not
with a lard knife. His guilty thought had had takers
and here they were at it.

And the rest got off & somehow here he swings
in the open air of an Edinburgh morning
for an impulse of mercy.
Who's good, who's evil, whose tail or whose wings
crosses his failing mind. The stop was mourning
and it was all well done.

When in the flashlights' flare the adultering pair
sat up with horror under the crab-apple tree
(soon to be hacked away for souvenirs)
and with their breasts & brains waited, & with ears
while masked & sheeted figures silently—
'Kneel, I-love,' he stammered, 'and pray,' Henry was there.

When four shots snapped, one for the Reverend,
her sick howl, three for her, in the heads, all fatal, and
when her throat is slit so deep the backbone eddies,
her worshipful foolish letters strewn between the bodies,
her tongue & voice-box out, his calling card
tipped up by his left heel, Henry was toward.

When to the smokeless mild celestial air
they came reproved & forgiven, her soul hurrying after his,
when bright with wisdom of the risen Lord
enthroned, they swam toward where what may be IS
and with the rest Mrs Mills, larynx & tongue restored,
choiring Te Deum, Henry was not there.

# Henry's Programme for God

'It was not gay, that life.' You can't 'make me small,'
you can't 'put me down' or take away my job.
I am immune,
although it is not gay. Why did we come at all,
consonant to whose bidding? Perhaps God is a slob,
playful, vast, rough-hewn.

Perhaps God resembles one of the last etchings of Goya
& not Valesquez, never Rembrandt no.
Something disturbed,
ill-pleased, & with a touch of paranoia
who calls for this thud of love from his creatures-O.
Perhaps God ought to be curbed.

Not only on this planet, I admit; somewhere.
*Our* only resource is bleak denial or
anti-potent rage,
both have been tried by our wisest. Who was it back there
who died unshriven, daring to see what more
could happen to a painter with such courage?

# 239

Am I a bad man? Am I a good man?
—Hard to say, Brother Bones. Maybe you both,
like most of we.
—The evidence is difficult to structure towards deliberate evil.
But what of the rest? Does it wax for wrath
in its infinite complexity?

She left without a word, for Ecuador.
I would have liked to discuss more with her this thing
through the terrible nights.
She was than Henry wiser, being younger or
a woman. She brought me Sanka and violent drugs
which were yet wholly inadequate.

My doctor doubles them daily. Am I a bad one—
I'm thinking of them fires & their perplexness—
or may a niche be found
in nothingness for completely exhausted Henry?
But it comes useless to canvass this alone,
out of her eyes and sound.

Air with thought thick, air scratched. The desks are hinged,
I foresee, for storing. And when a while has changed
(the people are hinged too,
for storing) . . . But now they are taking our exams
and the great room is busy with still Damns.
The proctor's hinged & blue,

that's me. The desks come out (I come not out)
each August on the mountain and bear thought.
I feel they do not mind.
I don't know. Maybe the gross creation howls
with storage & returns. Rings full of towels
wheel, both fighters are blind,

nobody passes, neither—of all—at length
Miss Jewell's eyes & Mr Torrey's strength.
My rafters bulge with death
kindly arising from creaking bodies, from
my hundreds braining & self-burdensome
yawning down there, catching their breath.

Father being the loneliest word in the one language
and a word only, a fraction of sun & guns
'way 'way ago,
on a hillside, under rain, maneuvers, once,
at big dawn. My field-glasses surpass—he sang—
yours.

Wicked & powerful, shy Henry     lifted his head with an offering.
Boots greeted him & it.
I raced into the bank,
my bank, after two years, with healthy cheques
& nobody seem to know me: was I ex-:
like Daddy??

O. O . . . I can't help feel I lift' the strain,
toward bottom. Games is somewhat too, but yet
certains improve
as if upon their only. We grinned wif wuv
for that which each of else was master of.
Christen the fallen.

About that 'me.' After a lecture once
came up a lady asking to see me. 'Of course.
When would you like to?'
Well, *now*, she said. 'Yes, but I have a lunch-
eon—' Then I saw her and shifted with remorse
and said 'Well; come on over.'

So we crossed to my office together and I sat her down
and asked, as she sat silent, 'What is it, miss?'
'Would you close the door?'
Now Henry was perplexed. We don't close doors
with students; it's just a principle. But this
lady looked beyond frown.

So I rose from the desk & closed it and turning back
found her in tears—apologizing—'No,
go right ahead,' I assur-
ed her, 'here's a handkerchief. Cry.' She did, I did. When she got
    control, I said 'What's the matter—if you want to talk?'
'Nothing. Nothing's the matter.' So.
I am her.

An undead morning. I . . . shuffle my poss's.
Lashed here, with ears, in the narrows, memoried,
like a remaining man,
he call to him for discomfort blue-black losses,
gins & green girls, drag of the slaying weed.
Just when it began again

I will remember, soon. All will be, soon.
The little birds are crazed. Survive us, gulls.
A hiss from distant space
homes in the overcast—to their grown tune—
dead on my foaming galley. Feel my pulse.
Is it the hour to replace my face?

Dance in the gunwales to what they cannot hear
my lorn men. I bear every piece of it.
Often, in the ways to come,
where the sun rises and fulfils their fear,
unlashed, I'll whistle bits.
Through the mad Pillars we are bound for home.

Calamity Jane lies very still
her soles to Wild Bill's skull
whose sudden guns are gone
The pike what leapt is trash
a sun-discoloured flash she lookt on
that time    That time is gone

Gold seen soils the whild hills
the braided sky    A woman is kinder
Her gun was not his own
In girdle & bra go forth to war & mines
her horse (Ha! ha!) is whiffs of bone
All that was heat lightning & one vivid blunder

Turning I see in silk & pearl
pliant while the gale does down
in the canyons of summer cold
Jane, Middleton's girl,
Yankee ladies, Joan—behold
with a hot sigh they lie down

# 245

# *A Wake-Song*

*(K's first administration seen in the light of the relevant history)*

Find me a sur-vivid fool, find me another
able to run the first, find me two fools
with an absence of skills
and each must do precisely sublimely the same
& pry on each other, under,—and lest this be seen
let there in their offices sub-fools

with sub-fools interfere: doing aught else—
(there is a work called *The Republic*): over them set
an Ivy appointee
who knows about from no   & nowhere; also then
let the elected officials (none though in jail)
diarrhea about Democracy,

starting with the Harlem vicer. By a friction-vote
barely let Boston millions in, dies the opponent
(in public opinion,
the crude of the 'papers). Keep on doing that.
I personally have voted Democratic all my life
and hate foreign ideas.

1) Our contempt for our government is mildly traditional, as represented by the communistic fascists Mark Twain, Stephen Crane, Edmund Wilson, and other maddogs.
2) Anyone's professional experience with our officials moronic will instruct him. Although with a lawyer's stupidity they cannot get a date right, their demands are Pharaoh's, until you make them cringe; whom we support, whose servants they purport to be.

Flaps, on winter's first day, loosely the flag
across thorns, a thorny tree like a sniper,
like our enthusiasm,
and the spread asylum in a spirit's
which we don' call it. Henry too drifts sag—after
what time his baby borns.

Ten feeding big birds treating with contempt
Sir squirrel, with lazy flaps of 18 inches;
Henry they do not like,
& leave. His morning's not one the sun skimpt,
woods mild & freckled below Geriatrics.
Our old set of cinches

seem to 've come down in the world—what's the phrase,
I haven't drunk a drink in 7 days,
they're in a flap, a bind, almost but not quite free.
To each blow something new crunched.
I wish my girl would out. The old man hunched
blind-sober on his porch like me.

Henry walked as if he were ashamed
of being in the body. This did not last
forever him
but many of his moments best on it he blamed;
so complex, man. He rooted in our past,
his future shrinking slim.

'His Majesty, the Body' Kafka wrote
a terrible half-truth. Visions of beauty drew
all him from his affairs,
O treacherous eyes! On a transatlantic boat
a lady seen not met ran him like the crew
& Captain. Thicker fears

condensed on him like ice, should he meet her.
A tiger watches from a vector. Ah,
watch we that tiger back,
and chance is King, a jacket lined with fur
for June, while viruses in the back seat clamour
for the whole man glowing black.

Snowy of her breasts the drifts, I do believe,
although I have not been there. Mild her voice
and often for no reason secrecies.
A healthy peasant out of this might weave
an ugly story, when we might rejoice
but let's not bother. For size,

she's medium. She is no mathematician.
Nor is Henry, and in that they're one.
Of other congruence
we'll less say. The sky begins to blond
this tiger-lily here in Sarah's pot
blonds, with the consequences

Dream on of a private life but you won't make it
Your fated life is public, lest we cheer,
take it easy, kid.
You lie uneasy whom we all endear
where storms come down from the mountains
The dog a rug away is munching a bone.

Bushes lay low. Uneven grass even lay low.
(The parking lot was tranquil.) Great sky hung dark.
We hurried. A spattering
pursued us to the orange old Chevrolet
and I was off to spit a double lecture,
tired in the cortex, flat

out but upright, wise with notes. I love storms;
I loathe this wisdom Henry gives of. Help?
Yes, to the attentive children,—
who only, at twenty, into each other's arms
would care to be confided, but don't dare
and who are neither men

nor not, nor women not. And sixty do not care
and they are bored with the electrifying air
& the Don & thunder-claps.
And I am bored. That's a lie. But six are wild
quietly for the question of the length of the hairs
on the mole of his girl. Child,

sád sights. A crumpled, empty cigarette pack.
O empty bottle. Hey: an empty girl.
Fill 'er up, pal.
I cough my proper blood. A time advances, black
& full? when I won't hafta. Seconal: . . .
no. Let's put the road on the show.

As folk-talk (what we have for proverbs) swirl
the valid & a mad; yeah, mad, and so
the valid, man.
Often I had to mutter what hurt an'
(while sunsets rose in the clothes of the field of God)
what kin hurt on . . .

I fit the holster. I was not sight-seein'.
I loved her and she killed me. That be so.
I killed her all, too.
The ability of sleep leaves you forever. Odd.
So musing, they blew the whistle on The Cat
which was that.

# *Walking, Flying—I*

Henry wandered: west, south, north, and East,
sometimes for money, sometimes for relief,
sometimes of pure fatigue,
sometimes a stroller through the mental feast
found him at Schwetzingen or Avila
or the Black Hills in Dakota,

found him in bizarre Tangier or outside Dublin
or inside the Palais des Papes at Avignon
where the guide suddenly sang
to show off the acoustics or in the Lakes to relax.
He admired the fantastic airway into Hong Kong
all circling peaks & waters,

and sweated in the airport appertaining to Bangkok;
but mostly travel is missing, by a narrow margin,
things desired: Elephanta,
the Badlands; once a dinner fellow-guest & I
reckoned up merely what each missed during his months in India:
together we made the whole subcontinent sigh.

# *Walking, Flying—II*

We hit the great cities (only I missed Madras),
*He* missed Bhuvaneshwar & Pataliputra
without having seen which
one can scarcely claim one visited the land.
One-down-manship we practiced: Konarak both missed,
for diverse & trivial & fatal

reasons. Besides, he was travelling. I was working,
on loan from the State Department,
Henry, less unreliable O than they,
doing it again I'd do it at a saunter, like
Old Ben in Paris, when as we were young
& our country regarded as a tyke.

Travel's a plague. But that's no matter. So is home.
It's paying out cash everyday that actually bugs you.
Isn't getting rid of old friends
worth it? And the destruction of mail en route
worth anything? Accompanies the combers foam
into which we dive too.

# *Walking, Flying—III*

He shopped down Siaghin, and through Sierpes,
threading Chandni-Chauk he brought off coups,
with the Champs-Elysées likewise
was Henry not unfamiliar: as of antiques
& rare books he murmured 'Whose?'
O he askt little questions & glanced at the eyes
of the avid seller, sior.

That was in Venice. Once to me in Venice
a man told a fact. I lookt into his eyes
and I saw he wanted less:
I found myself in a position to check this fact
but didn't: life is hard enough for everybody:
Honour wanders: I bought it.

On John R st. in Detroit he made a bargain.

He has been shopping around the streets of the world
decades & woes—and how does he show for it?
'Ashes, ashes. All fall *down*.'
Siaghin was nothing. It was into the Casbah
at midnight where he was truly taken,
out of his prone for products.

Mrs Thomas, Mrs Harris, and Mrs Neevel
were all his students all a summer's day.
He couldn't tell, from the other, one.
And he did teach them Luther, who undone
the sacramental system & taught evil
is *ingrained*. Why,

that was a sexy summer, with Mrs Thomas
sitting under her hair on a chair-form
& Mrs Harris & Mrs Neevel
who I may hope for Mr Harris & Mr Neevel
do giant shrimp in olive oil & lemon
taking no notes.

Mrs T, Mrs H & Mrs N
figured among my kids, busy as all
get-out, in our shrewd heat.
Luther went into seclusion, along with Mrs Thomas,
and once I felt in my flying     tackle face a cleat
when I sailed through the Fifth Form.

My twin, the nameless one, wild in the woods
whilst I at Pippin's court flourish, am knighted:
we met & fighted
on a red road, made friends, and all my goods
now are half his. I pull this out of the past,
St Valentine's forecast.

Trim, the complex lace, whitest on red:
my baby's kindergarten had a ball
save one got none at all
& tears, like those for the Roman martyr shed
& the bishop of Terni who suffered the same day,
so ancient writers say.

I say, said Henry (all degrees of love
from sky-blue down to spiriting blood, down to
the elder from the new,
loom sanctuaries we are pilgrims of,
the pierced heart over there seems to be mine)
this is my Valentine.

Henry rested, possessed of many pills
& gin & whiskey. He put up his feet
& switched on Schubert.
His tranquillity lasted five minutes
for (1) all that undone all the heavy weeks
and (2) images shook him alert.

A rainy Sunday morning, on vacation
as well as Fellowship, he could not rest:
bitterly he shook his head.
—Mr Bones, the Lord will bring us to a nation
where everybody only rest. —I confess
that notion bores me dead,

for there's no occupation there, save God,
if that, and long experience of His works
has not taught me his love.
His love must be a very strange thing indeed,
considering its products. No, I want rest here,
neither below nor above.

The thunder & the flaw of their great quarrel
abased his pen. He could not likely think.
He took himself out of it,
both wrong & right, beyond well beyond moral,
in the groves of meaningless rage, which ache & stink
unlike old shit

which loses its power almost in an hour,
ours burgeons. When I trained my wives, I thought
now they'll be professional:
they became professional, at once wedlocks went sour
because they couldn't compete with Henry, who sought
their realizations. The J.P. coughed.

Married life is a boat
forever dubious, with the bilge stale.
There's no getting out of that.
Gongs & lightning crowd my returned throat,
I always wept at parades: I knew I'd fail:
Henry wandered back on stage & sat.

Scarlatti spurts his wit across my brain,
so too does *Figaro:* so much for art
after the centuries yes
who had for all their pains above all pain
& who brought to their work a broken heart
but not as bad as Schubert's:

that went beyond the possible: that was like a man
dragged by his balls, singing aloud 'Oh yes'
while to his anguisht glance
the architecture differs: he's getting on,
the tops of buildings change, like a mad dance,
the Piazza Navona

recovers its calm after he went through,
the fountain went on splashing, all was the same
after his agony,
abandoned cats had what to say to you,
lovers performed their glory & its shame:
Henry put his foot down: free.

Does then our rivalry extend beyond
your death? our lovely friendly rivalry
over a quarter-century?
One of my students gives me, late, a long paper
on one of your poems, which I barely can stand
for excellence & loss?

When worst it got, you went away I charge you
and we will wonder over this in Hell
if the circles communicate.
I stayed here. It's changing from blue to blue
but you would be rapt with the gold hues, well,
you went like Pier to another fate,

I never changed. My desire for death was strong
but never strong enough. I thought: this is my chance,
I can bear it.
I'm not a Buddhist. I studied the systems long,
the High Systems. Come hunt me, ancient friend,
and tell me I am wrong.

Tides of dreadful creation rocked lonely Henry
isolated in the midst of his family
as solitary as his dog.
In another world he'll have more to say of this,—
concepts came forward & were greeted with a kiss
in the passionate fog.

Lucid his project lay, beyond. Can he?
Loose to the world lay unimaginable Henry,
loose to the world,
taut with his vision as it has to be,
open & closed sings on his mystery
furled & unfurled.

Flags lift, strange chords lift to a climax. Henry
is past. Returning from his travail, he
can't think of what to say.
The house's all about him, so is his family.
Tame doors swing upon his mystery
until another day.

Restless, as once in love, he put pen to paper—
a stub point with real ink, he hates ballpoints—
and on a thick pad, on lap—
how many thousands times has this been the caper,
in fear & love, with interest, whom None anoints,
taking instead the fourth rap—

habitual—life sentence—will he see it through?
or will a long vac, at the end of time—
discharge—greet gravid Henry?
Many a one his pen's been bad unto,
which they deserved, some honoured in his rhyme
which they deserved, hee hee!

A stub point: *one* odd way to Paradise
ha ha! but of more dignity than my typewriter,
than my marvellous pencils darker.
We're circling, waiting for the tower & the marker
the radio's out, some runways are brighter
as we break Control & come down with our size.

The tenor of the line of your retreats,
done in an instant, hurts me forever. Well,
I suffer that bad will
so long as I suffer. You    would not have wanted this,
the chaining of your friend to your abyss
with one of the best seats.

I overlook the hopeless spectacle
with pity & love & almost    perfect admiration,
I feel your terror.
I wish I didn't. Go, but not to hell
but you have disqualified yourself for this nation
of attempts & trial-&-error.

You lowered a wall between us
which was your privilege. Now you must not expect
anything but suffering more,
fearless & final. You became anonymous
and untruth after in your regard will be correct
hung on the veil you tore.

## 2 6 3

You couldn't bear to grow old, but we grow old.
Our differences accumulate. Our skin
tightens or droops: it alters.
Take courage, things are not what they have been
and they will never again. Hot hearts grow cold,
the rush to the surface falters,

secretive grows the disappearing soul
learned & uncertain, young again
but not in the same way:
Heraclitus had a wise word here to say,
which I forget. We wake & blunder on,
wiser, on the whole,

but not more accurate. Leave that to the young,
grope forward, toward where no one else has been
which is our privilege.
Besides, you gave up early in our age
which is your privilege, from Chatterton
to the bitter & present scene.

I always wanted to be old, I wanted to say
'O I haven't read that for fifteen years'
or 'my copy of that
seems in the usual course to have gone astray'
or 'She—that woman moved me to young tears,
even Henry Cat.'

But now the moment's mine, I find I love it not.
Base envy of the very young afflicts me,
contempt & boredom, but envy.
I just came on my notes for an old play,
fifty volumes I read from Widener, thought
that now would turn me grey

roiled in my burning brain, Connolly & Pearse
my hero-martyrs over fifty books
stampt down in lime:
their triumph needs a man younger in rhyme,
reservationless, unfeeling for the worse,
a young man with three rooks.

I don't know one damned butterfly from another
my ignorance of the stars is formidable,
also of dogs & ferns
except that around my house one destroys the other
When I reckon up my real ignorance, pal,
I mumble 'many returns'—

next time it will be nature & Thoreau
this time is Baudelaire if one had the skill
and even those problems O
At the mysterious urging of the body or Poe
reeled I with chance, insubordinate & a killer
O formal & elaborate I choose you

but I love too the spare, the hit-or-miss,
the mad, I sometimes can't     always tell them apart
As we fall apart, will you let me hear?
That would be good, that would be halfway to bliss
You said will you answer back? I cross my heart
& hope to die but not this year.

Dinch me, dark God, having smoked me out.
Let Henry's ails fail, pennies on his eyes
never to open more,
the shires are voting him out of time & place,
they'll drop his bundle, drunkard & Boy Scout,
where he was once before:

nowhere, nowhere. Was then the thing all planned?
I mention what I do not understand.
I mention for instance Love:
God loves his creatures when he treats them so?
Surely one grand *exception* here below
his presidency of

the widespread galaxies might once be made
for perishing Henry, whom let not then die.
He can advance no claim,
save that he studied thy Word & grew afraid,
work & fear be the basis for his terrible cry
not to forget his name.

Can Louis die? Why, then it's time to join him
again, for another round, the lovely man.
Years roll away,
and we are back in London, in '53.
He was doing the documentary
of the Everest film.

(Book V is done. Would Louis have been delighted therewith?)
He was not of the character of myth,
& knew nothing about climbing.
I had to tell him about Leigh-Mallory
& Leigh-Mallory's daughter Clare, & Leigh-Mallory's
remark: 'Because it is there.'

So Henry's thought rushed onto a thousand screens
& Louis', the midwife of it. A thousand dreams behind,
birds are incredibly stupid.
My love for Louis transcended his good work,
and—older than Henry—saw him not in the dark
& suffocating.

2 6 8

Henry, absent on parade, hair-triggered, mourned
on Memorial Day a many of my dead
and all of the living.
He finally decided: It's forgiving.
We wakes at dawn & we sits up, forlorned,
besides the panic dread.

His love passed on to him through one a note,
which made him ache. Notes in the sullen ground
are not passed, or found.
Their solitude is great & dug to last,
their final memory the scary boat.
Now let's have a new sound:

that of the banners & the bands, and my love,
in triumphant reckoning: they die, we cheer,
Hurrah for the lost!
These thoughts, and of his love, in his mind he tossed
enough until he nearly died thereof.
Then came back the fear.

Acres of spirits every single day
shook headed Henry toward his friendly grave.
But after one square mile
less he shook, more he laboured, with each Wave
further he vanished, while the great sky grew grey
never to wake again while

the visible universe grows older, while
onflying stars out to my edges sail—
the edges of what?
I pause in a welcome distance of applauses
Henry obeyed sometimes some strange old laws:
mostly he made his own, cupshot.

High weird the hymns now in his final days,
items he sought of what was once called praise
which now spits & shrieks,
They say Henry's love is well beyond Henry
& advise the poor man back into the tree
giving up spirits & steaks.

This fellow keeps on sticking at his drum,
the only decent german for decades. Some
would like you to make room,
mother, and you know where
whence we were foxed to flower into power
& bloom, headed thence for the tomb.

Womb was the word, where Henry never developed.
Prudent of him, though gloomy. I assume
that which you neglect.
The face he put on matters, slightly wrecked,
passed muster O at noon & while he supped
& enroute back to the womb.

There was no time, in the end, to finish her off.
Halfway he left her, with the right side of her head
a' gone,
with the strength to speak diminishing instead
but cured forever of that coffin cough
& the rest of her hair wind-blown.

Why then did he make, at such cost, *crazy* sounds?
to waken ancient longings, to remind (of childness),
to make laugh, and to hurt,
is and was all he ever intended. Short
came his commands.
Today, in April, the clouds have personalities. Yes,

there's a lamb one; that's lying down; he waits
his frightful chances; she hangs over; there's a dove;
two are conspiring;
one flies, wild. These banks and ranks of glowing cloud require
his passioning attention. Throng the Fates,
he couldn't care less, being in love

with his own teeming lady,—whose dorsal fin
is keeping her nauseous. Wait till that kid
comes out, I'll fix her.
I'll burp her till she bleeds, I'll take an ax
to her inability to focus, until in
one weird moment I fall in love with her too.

The subject was her. He was the object. Clings
still to these facts affect. If little cats
come to the parapet
and hurt my shoulders, growing there like wings
where most I should go safe: let's face it, that's
the looking to a wet.

—I'll see you in the a.m., Dr Bones.
—Don't leave now. An eminence of man,
an imminence of her,
boils on my brothers' deaths. Nobody owns
much, good friend. A parapet with wings,
an egg lined with fur.

—I really gotta go. You don' make sense.
—I don't try to. Get with it. When's said & done
all that we did & said
& drank & dreamt, a hundred seasons hence,
who'll forgive sunspots & the stains of the son
where all we crawled & bled?

Survive—exist—who is at others' will
optionless; may gelded be, be put to stud,
and were sweating sold;
was sold. —Mr Bones, dat slavey still
is of our former coast. —When they make me, Bud,
I show my genitals, cold.

Saudi Arabia is *mah* favourite place.
'conditioned Cadillacs, like bigoty Texas
of our own mindless oil.
Come closer, Sambo. I planting in your face
ilex. Your face. You jus like a flex
where the bulb failed. Flail

upon Bahrein, at one hundred-odd degrees
at four in the morning, where the ofays' cameras
were dutyless.—
Muscle my whack. We gotta trickle. Seize
them Moslem testicles, and pull. Please
hurt my owner, twice.

# 274

It's lovely just here now in the midst of night:
cool. I take back some of my imprecations,
some. I turn the fan off.
The twenty-score people who count on me for tomorrow
probably will be satisfied. Maybe I will.
The summer has been rough,

I've booked our passage to a greener scene
and there my soul is earning. My insulted body
though still is earning here.
My o'ertaxed brain, in its units, hangs on between.
It even keeps an office hour, a strange lady
rang up today to know when.

We'll do our best for the lady and the hundreds
and we will do our best for the cause of the brain
though sea-foam tugs
eastward my heart, my manuscripts are ready
for transport, and suddenly it all seems quite sane
to a man who has rolled up the rugs.

## July 11

And yet I find myself able, at this deep point,
to carry out my duties: I lecture, I write.
I am even lecturing well,
I threw two chairs the janitors had piled
on the podium to the floor of the lecture hall:
the students were amazed

it was good for them, action in the midst of thought,
an angry Zen touch, something not written down
except in the diaries
of the unknown devoted ones of the 115:
'Master Henry is approaching his limit.'
A little more whiskey please.

A little more whiskey please. Something's gotta give
either in edgy Henry or the environment:
the conflict cannot last,
I soothe myself with, though for 50 years
the war's made headlines. Waiting for fall
and the cold fogs thereof
                              in delicious Ireland.

# Henry's Farewell—I

He tossed a farewell party for his pals
who all at once sat up to groom their wives
to California's airs,
leaving Henryville bereft, carnivals-
cum-intellect closed down now, off in pairs
they flew to lead fresh lives

alas, which was their perfect right, alas.
Henry repaired to Dublin, showing his back,
to thrive on shanty-talk.
'*They'll* miss *me* too' he muttered, and 'A sorry pass,
when the best are so dispersed one has to chalk
up thousands of miles for one crack

or canny reference' shaking his head he groaned
and grinned at his green friends across his stout
but his heart was not in it, his heart was out
with the loss of friends now to be telephoned
only when drunk and at enormous cost:
he gnashed out a lonesome toast.

# Henry's Farewell—II

Willing them well! He hoped would not collapse
at once their institutions new, and houses.
*His* was firm enough.
He'd look for them hereafter on his maps,
with wives' details in letters: Henry loved,
a scholar who swoops, who browses,

the daily far routine of all his friends
living, and he grew very good at it:
coward is high by ten,
mostly by noon the poets have made amends
and downed their guilt toward that of other men,
O and far scholars sit

baffled or flourish! You're for better jobs,
I bless you in their outcomes, with a Liffey grin:
Henry is out, you're in,
long-term: spark him a formula for mobs
you'll tally no more: here's to your tiny classes
tanned lads & opulent lasses
    and therefore all your grand works we'll see win

# Henry's Farewell—III

Fail may your enemies, abundant here,
in that most happy clime. Play it by ear
out there until all's straight
and may no rudeness interrupt your play.
One decade's war forget, in which, I may say,
we've scarcely won a battle to this date.

Fresh from the woodwork issued our blue foes
botanists & peasants of elementary german
drones, drones in the hive
Faction ran wild & so did many vermin
fresh from their woodwork and we bore their blows
& carried on our work alive.

I fear the queen is swarming, toward the west
taking her chosen workers, for a stunt
leaving behind her Henry.
No harm in that, the old survival test.
Pardon my sore toast, nominal & blunt
& let's get on toward the sea.

# VII

Leaving behind the country of the dead
where he must then return & die himself
he set his tired face due East
where the sun rushes up the North Atlantic
and where had paused a little the war for bread
& the war for status had ceased

forever, and he took with him five books,
a Whitman & a Purgatorio,
a one-volume dictionary,
an Oxford Bible with all its bays & nooks
& bafflements long familiar to Henry
& one other new book-O.

If ever he had crafted in the past—
but only if—he swore now to craft better
which lay in the Hands above.
He said: I'll work on slow, O slow & fast,
if a letter comes I will answer that letter
& my whole year will be tense with love.

Decision taken, Henry'll be back abroad,
from where things look more inter'sting, where things
American are seen
without America's perpetual self-laud
as if everything in America had wings,
the world else a crawling scene,

the world else peripheral. Now good London crimes,
Irish & Spanish sports, Japanese disasters
will leave him free to think.
He'll still have bad ol' *Time* each week, & *The Times*,
to clue him in to the actions of his masters.
He bought a lot of ink,

having much to say, masterless after all, & gay
with probability, time being on his side,
the large work largely done,
over the years, the prizes mostly won,
we work now for ourself alone, away
even from pal & wife, in ways not to be denied.

# The Following Gulls

We missed Quebec but now the North Shore lights
are bright against the lowered clouds of dusk,
they come in two broad bands,
neither of which was ever before in Henry's sights,
and he is preparing not for strangeness but
familiarity's demands.

The manic glare with which these passengers
took in one another is diminishing
into routine,
I have made my first acquaintance and one steward
has revealed to me his secret in Florida & Duluth
& London.

After thirty Falls I rush back to the haunts of Yeats
& others, with a new book in my briefcase
four times too large:
all year I must in terminal debates
with me say who is to lives & who to dies
before my blessed discharge.

Richard & Randall, & one who never did,
two who will never cross this sea again,
& Delmore,
filled his pitted mind as the ship forged on
I hear the three freaks in their different notes
discussing more & more

our meaning to the Old World, theirs to us
which much we pondered in our younger years
and then coughed & sang
the new forms in which ancient thought appears
the altering bodies of the labile souls,
foes fang on fang.

The lovely friends, and friends the friends of friends,
pursuing insights to their journeys' ends
subtle & steadfast:
the wind blows hard from our past into our future
and we are that wind, except that the wind's nature
was not to last.

Shrouded the great stars, the great boat moves on.
A minimum of tremor in the bar.
Today was Children's Day
& the Little Twiss prinked out ah as a bunny
won or did not win—I forget—second prize:
I forget to say.

I forget the great ship steaming thro' the dark
I forget the souls *so* eager for their pain.
Two have just dropt in,
grand ships' officers, large heads & gold braid,
the authority of the bartender is dwarfed
I forget all the old

I seem to be Henry then at twenty-one
steaming the sea again      in another British boat
again, half mad with hope:
with my loved Basque friend I stroll the topmost deck
high in the windy night, in love with life
which has produced this wreck.

The hand I shook will operate no more
after forty years of cutting. We admire
the blossoms of youth
on the tall English boys.
The sun roars on the sea today. The old are fat.
These handsome raucous ones are said to be Rhodes scholars.

On the whole boat one passenger knows my name
& that's too many. Fog has all the sea
we drive on purposeful.
Henry is one of the three passengers
who is doing any work. Grins given strangers
diminish his isolation.

But now he lies in the golden sun & eats.
Fun & games, the fresh acquaintances,
with a heavy heart.
Wide sported the sea behind, the land of art
lay off ahead far: meanwhile chats & dances,
trivial triumphs, defeats.

Much petted Henry like a petal throve,
his narthex let the girls & pupils in,
aptotic he remained
Henry's own man, when he squirmed not in love,
fifty pressures herded one discipline:
the sun shot up, it rained,

weathering Henry kept on his own side,
whatever in the name of God that side was.
And he struggled, pal.
Apricate never: too he took in his stride
more than most monsters can. Whatever the cause
they called him Madrigal

and Introit, passing him on the road
wherever they were going and were gone.
Henry peered quite alone
as if the worlds would answer to a code
just around the corner, down gelid dawn,
beckoning like a moan.

So Henry's enemy's lost, not paranoia
but cancer, long. I would him very well,
forgetful or choiring,
whether the Great One is hiring or firing.
Stationed there permanent, does he enjoy a
bell for Mass, for matrimony, the passing bell?

Henry walked the corridor in dark, drug-drunk, smoking
and dropt it & near-sighted cannot find.
Nurses will deal hell if the ward wakes, croaking
to smoke antic with flame.
All the parts of this damned floor are the same.
He scrabbled, worried hard, with half his mind.

Like the breakfast bell on fire
it brings O ho it brings around again
what miserable Henry must desire:
aplomb
at the temps
of the tomb.

A best word across a void makes a hard blaze.
Henry reacted like a snake to praise,
he shed his skin
appearing thenceforward in a new guise
so the praise was for     his past, he not therein,
saving him from vanity, the mirror's eyes,

saving him from greed. Lean as a snake
he staked his claim upon obscurity:
a prayer to be left alone
escaped him sometimes or for a middle zone
where he could be & become both unknown & known,
listening & not.

A flower a year, enough to grieve him on, to the extent that one
     is able,
from absolutely certain wits, he was pleased with
& one has just now come,
an unexpected & triumphing cable
when least he hoped for hope, & most needed it,
making him feel at home.

In neighbourhoods evil of noise, he deployed, Henry,
stance unheroic. Say yes without offending.
In our career here
good will we too with ill. Wrinkle a grin.
The place is not so bad, considering
the alternative with real fear.

Being dead, I mean. 'Well it is a long rest'
to himself said Mr Bloom. But is it that now?
As one Hungarian
Jew to another, I have seen grins that test
our patience, pal. Things are getting out
of hand, gaffered another one.

Blundering, faltering, uphill all the way
& icy. O say yes without offending.
His heart, a mud-puddle, sang.
'Serve, Serve' it sang, and it sang that all day.
New tasks will craze you in your happy ending.
Let go without a pang.

It is, after all her! & in the late afternoon
of the last day! & she is even more delightful
than longing Henry expected:
Parisienne, bi-lingual, teaches English,
at 27 unmarried, for she has not found
anyone 'not ordinary':

(another couple in the Club have come to terms)
on this last day she is more beautiful high-coloured
even than Henry's wife
who is pale, pale & beautiful: Yvette's ankles
are slim as the thought of various poets I could mention
& she tilts her head proudly.

'Twould not be possible for her to lose her dignity,
I notice this at dusk in a rising sea,
such an excellent lady
I will have more to say at a later time
with my whole cracked heart, in prose or rhyme
of this lady of the northern sea.

Why *is* Ireland the wettest place on earth
year-round, beating Calcutta in the monsoon
& the tropical rain-forest?
Clearly the sun has made an exception for Ireland,
the sun growled & shone elsewhere: Iowa,
detestable State.

Adorable country, in its countryside
& persons, & its habits, & its past,
martyrs & heroes,
its noble monks, its wild men of high pride
& poets long ago, Synge, Joyce & Yeats,
and the ranks from which they rose.

Detestable State, made of swine & corn,
rich & ignorant, pastless, with one great tree in it
& doubtless certain souls
perplexed as the Irish whether to shout or mourn
over man's riddling fate: alter, or *stet:*
Fate across all them rolls.

Cold & golden lay the high heroine
in a wilderness of bears. His spirit fled
upon this apparition.
She never moved but the bears were moved to move
and if he could have been sure that she was dead
he would have fled for all his love

leaving behind him fractured vows, for he loathed bears.
Their giant forelegs & their terrible paws
not to mention their teeth, theirs
Like an old sabre-tooth tiger's famished & wild
hurling himself upon a mastodon
and gorging, reconciled.

Just once, the tiger wondered to itself:
I am their enemy, I have enemies
almost as bad as Fr. Rolfe;
friendship is *out*. How then can we administer our affairs
in the absence of slaves & stewards, if you please,
who may hire us for theirs.

The Irish sky is raining, the Irish winds are high,
the Irish sun comes back & forth, and I
in my Irish pub
past puberty & into pub-erty
have sent my Irish wife & child downtown,
I lapse like an Irish clown.

I dream, and God knows Henry's dreams are vivid
as the horses in Poona, lustrous on the track
whose father will not swim back
ruined in a grave in Oklahoma
loveless except for Henry steept in Homer
& *Timon* & livid.

Henry, who was always a crash programme,
smiled, and the smile was worse than the rictus of the victim,
'Another drop' said Mick.
He put his silver down, he took back all his lies,
he went down chimneys under the Irish skies
& the last voice in drawled; 'Henry? a brick,'

What gall had he in him, so to begin Book VII
or to design, out of its hotspur materials,
its ultimate structure
whereon will critics browse at large, at Heaven Eleven
finding it was not cliffhangers or old serials
but according to his nature

O the baby has had one million & thirteen falls,
no wonder she howls
She'll trip on the steps at Vassar, ho, & bawl
in Latin. That baby has got to learn things
including remaining erect & on deck & all,
her study of herself must include no wings.

She's sturdy, beautiful, & she will do, unless
the universal homage turns her head
as it well might do mine,
hyp*m*otized by the Little Baby, who has ears only for Diana & The
   Beast,
& mommy, & admirers & her Mir, instead
of brothers & sisters coming on like swine.

I broke a mirror, in which I figured you.
Henry did not lavish his hopes: he hoped to destroy
with this one act
the counter-forces against your art's design,
the burgeon of your heart. You have enemies,
my dear. It is a fact

that you have enemies: one word of praise
has grouped against you gangs against that word
of decent praise:
I urge you, with misgivings, on, these days,
the temperature of the end has not been taken,
so I have heard,

I trust your detestation of Carlyle
the evil way a genius can go.
I hope you hate Carlyle
& Emerson's insufferable essays,
wisdom in every line, while his wife cried upstairs,
disgusting Emerson & Rilke.

You dear you, clearing up Henry's foreign affairs,
with your sword & armour heading for his bank,
a cable gone astray:
except for you he had hopped in the Liffey & sank.
Now what can he in return do: upstairs? downstairs?
You run your life every day

*so* well it's hard to think      of anything you need
and I only supply needs, needs & ceremonies,
I'll send you the last thirteen,
in all of which Henry is extremely dead
but talkative. To you with your peat moss & leaf-mould
& little soft wet holes

where you put ginger, bloodroot & blueheads
& pearly everlasting,—what can he say of worth?
In all his nine lives
he was seldom so pleased been to be on the same earth
with you, my dear. We get on better than
most husbands & wives.

Of grace & fear, said Lady Valerie,
you are the master, Henry Pussy-cat.
After that a lovely silence,
the Lady sat there, away in Illinois,
Henry sat here, in Dublin's fair city,
close to Killarney Bay.

O that bay is excellent, the Atlantic is blue
and soon we'll take a plane across it to London,
Paris & Rome & Athens
& then, if all goes well, Jerusalem
where all those fine Jews are, & holy places
imperfectly determined.

O the sea is blue, & you are my honey dear,
purred Henry far away, in crisis. Fear
& grace, she suddenly said.
A sweet thing to say. Henry was a needer
of a very few or even of one reader
in the bright afternoon outspread.

Golden his mail came at his journey's end,
Henry was back in action. His old friend liked
his ancient sonnets,
and institutions had come up to scratch
awarding Henry much: now he was on his own,
no lectures, no seminars,

only the actual: I perfect my metres
until no mosquito can get through,
I love the Liffey,
ruined castles (three) make my blood flow
& that is what my doctor would contra-indicate
in my case.

Is there more to say? Surely I've said enough,
my mind has been laid open
for thirty years, as when I spoke of love
& either could not get it or had too much of it,
impenetrable Henry, goatish, reserved,
whose heart is broken.

Henry in transition, transient Henry,
rubbed his eyes & hurt. He was on TV
with his baby daughter,
and Housman's rhyme O in this case was 'oughter
and Henry did his bloody level best
for all them young Englishmen & so did his daughter.

The baby on a million screens, hurrah,
my almost perfect child, in the midst of the cameramen
& Daddy's high-lit reading.
She never made a peep to that sensitive mike
my born performer. We'll see her through Smith & then
swiftly into the Senate.

Daddy by then will be the nearest ghost,
honey, but won't return. Daddy's heart sank
at leaving the lovely baby.
Your Mommy will be with you, when Henry's a blank,
you'll have to study him in school, at most,
troubled & gone Henry.

The Irish have the thickest ankles in the world
& the best complexions. Unnerved by both,
Henry reserved his vote.
A dreadful dream, me stranded on a red rock slope
unable to go up, or down, or sideways:
shout for the Fire Department?

Your first day in Dublin is always your worst.
I just found my fly open: panic! A depressing
& badly written letter, very long,
from northern California enclosing a bad poem.
Fear of proving unworthy to my self-imposed task.
Fear.

And how will his last day in Dublin be,
away so many labours? —Offer up prayers,
Mr Bones. Down on your knees.
Life comes against     not all at once but in layers.
—You offers me this hope. Now I thank you,
depressed, down on my knees.

# Henry Comforted

*Your first day in Dublin is always your worst*
& today is better, as when thirty years ago
I recovered my spirits at once.
Unshaven, tieless, with the most expensive drink in the room,
I have recovered a little. The room is filling
with Irish types—one gorgeous girl,

pipe-men, cigarette-men, a portentous black beard,
& the accents are flying: the all-service man
is a giant with a shock of red hair & an easy air.
Henry is feeling better,
owing to three gin-&-vermouths.
He is seeking where to live & pursue his work.

The Irish are not neat, except in the Book of Kells.
The skirts are as short here as in Minnesota.
What the services need
is a teen-age H-bomb: fashions their elders can follow.
His shoes are momumental, Egyptian, ay
the two at my left are giving it verbal hell.

Shifted his mind &    was once more full of the great Dean
with his oddities about money & his enigmatic ladies,
the giant presences
chained to St Patrick's, tumultuous, serene,
their mighty stint done, larger in stone than life,
larger than Henry's belief

who now returns at fifty, conflict-scarred,
to see how they are doing: why, they are doing
just what thirty years ago
he thought they were doing, and it is not hard,
neither in doubt or trouble, neither gaining nor losing,
just being the same O.

His frantic huge mind left him long before the end,
he wandered mad through the apartments but once was seen
to pause by a shelf & look
at a copy of the *Tale of a Tub:* he took it down
& was heard to mutter 'What a genius was mine
when I wrote down that book.'

Cold & golden lay the high heroine
in a wilderness of bears. The forest tramped.
Henry was not at ease.
Intrusions had certainly been made on his dignities,
to his fury. Looking around, he felt cramped.
He said: This place is *theirs*,

I'll remove elsewhere, I will not live here
among my thugs. Lo, and he went away
to Dublin's fair city.
There he met at once two ladies dear
with problems, problems. Henry could not say
like their parish priest 'Pray'.

He immersed himself in their disabled fates
the catafalque above all for instance T—'s
and others' bound to come
The White House invitation came today,
three weeks after the reception, hey,
Henry not being at home.

# Three in Heaven I Hope

'Three in heaven I hope' said old Jane to Henry
'and one in a mental hospital and three wed.'
Henry had only three.
Jack's lounge roared around them    they chatted over their kids,
Ten-thirty. Work's over, except Henry's: more.
The Irish clouds outside giving us an Irish downpour.

The baby in her high & hurried voice
babbles while Henry rocks & rocks; aged four.
I do love that baby.
Of babies I have loved I declare I rejoice
chiefly in Paul & Martha, called Twissy-Pits,
and jack-knifed how on the floor she sits

doing her colouring & her scissoring.
Brought Jerry with me home last night, Kate got cross,
Jerry likes my baby too.
Working & children & pals are the point of the thing,
for the grand sea awaits us, which will then us toss
& endlessly us undo.

Maris & Valerie held his grand esteem
except for maybe Ellen on her hill-top
in northern California:
Maris the vividest writer yet, a team
not a woman, bringing bank mysteries to a stop,
relishing garden mysteries,

with the enigma of Boyd ever at her elbow
as Ellen has the enigma of Phil, while Valerie
has only & always her own
in her daring & placid beauty, which bestow
warily, my dear, warily, warily,
lest they want that alone.

I wrote to the White House yesterday, regretting
the lateness of an invitation there,
we couldn't accept:
I should have consulted him on my splendid getting
four ladies to write to Henry: who is most fair,
ingenious & adept?

Like the sunburst up the white breast of a black-footed penguin
amid infinite quantities of gin
Henry perceived his subject.
It came nearer, like a guilty bystander,
stood close, leaving no room to ponder,
Mickey Mouse & The Tiger on the table.

Leaving the ends aft open, touch the means,
whereby we ripen. Touch by all means the means
whereby we come to life,
enduring the manner for the matter, ay
I sing quickly, offered Henry, I
sing more quickly.

I sing with infinite slowness finite pain
I have reached into the corner of my brain
to have it out.
I sat by fires when I was young, & now
I'm not I sit by fires again, although
I do it more slowly.

The Danish priest has horns of solid fire
the angry little lady is for hire
Henry remembers it all
the steep-down street which also cost his ankle
His housemother Miss Dulon without a wrinkle
the long sweet days of Fall

the long sweet days of youths striving together
Friends so intense the world seems to hold no other
Henry remembers all
A night with a drunk B-girl & a drunk pawnbroker
They threw him out in the end, a half-drunk joker
whereas they went in her room on business

The green green fields between Cobh (Khōve) & Dublin
White horses grazing, most splendid since Kentucky
Henry remembers fire
Irish tenors impromptu in the Lounge
Thirty years of mostly labour & scrounge
The fire out of hand, the embers

The Irish monk with horns of solid mire
pillaged the countryside: Haw haw they cried
this is our favourite monk
He did them down dirty like a low-down skunk
The Irish sky remained fitful & wide
with clouds bright as fire

Helen or Henry is reborn in this place of the past
The Eighteenth Century lives on & on
Henry is overcome
with this solidity where shall he find a home?
The Irish converse about practical questions
& about finding us a house fast.

Cold & weary sought he a hearth, not just for now
but all the workful months to come, Adrienne
Succor me, be on my side
This is the chief lion-breeding place: I bow
gently to my superiors, being merely men
who have not been denied.

# An Instructions to Critics

The women of Kilkenny weep when the team loses,
they don't see the match but they cry. Mad bettors everywhere,
the sign "Turf Accountant",
men slipping in & out. People are all the same,
the seaman argued: Henry feels the Spanish & Irish
& Bengalis are thoroughly odd.

Americans, whom I prefer, are hopelessly normal.
The Japanese are barely comprehensible & formal,
formal Henry found.
We should have lowered the boom
on ourselves in our mother's womb,
dixit Henry's pal above ground.

My baby chatters. I feel the end is near
& strong of my large work, which will appear,
and baffle everybody.
They'll seek the strange soul, in rain & mist,
whereas they should recall the pretty cousins they kissed,
and stick with the sweet switch of the body.

Fallen leaves & litter. It is September.
Henry's months now begin. Much to be done
by merry Christmas,
much to be done by the American Thanksgiving
(I hate these English cigarettes), much to be done,
much to be done.

I went shopping today & came back with
a book about the Easter Rising, reality & myth—
all Henry's old heroes,
The O'Rahilly, Plunkett, Connolly, & Pearse,
spring back into action, fatuous campaigners
dewy with phantastic hope.

Phantastic hope rules Henry's war as well,
all these enterprises are doomed, all human pleas
are headed for the night.
Wait the lime-pits for all originators,
wounded propped up to be executed,
afterward known as martyrs.

His gift receded. He could write no more.
Be silent then, until the thing returns.
We have Goethe's warrant
for idling when no theme presents itself
or none that can be handled suitably:
I fall back on that high word.

I hate his race though, except Hölderlin
& Kleist, whom he clasped both to Henry's bosom:
a suicide & a madman,
to teach him lessons who was so far neither.
The language best handled by a foreigner,
Kafka, old pal.

Henry, monstrous bug, laid himself down
on the machine in the penal colony
without a single regret.
He was *all* regret, swallowing his own vomit,
disappointing people, letting everyone down
in the forests of the soul.

Famisht Henry ate everything in sight
after his ancient fast. His fasting was voluntary,
self-imposed.
He specially liked hunks of decent bread
sopped in olive-oil & cut raw onion,
specially.

Hunger was constitutional with him,
women, cigarettes, liquor, need need need
until he went to pieces.
The pieces sat up & wrote. They did not heed
their piecedom but kept very quietly on
among the chaos.

An old old mistress recently rang up,
here in Ireland, to see how Henry was:
how was he? delighted!
He thought she was 3000 miles away,
safe with her children in New York: she's coming at five:
we'll wélcome her!

## 312

I have moved to Dublin to have it out with you,
majestic Shade, You whom I read so well
so many years ago,
did I read your lesson right? did I see through
your phases to the real? your heaven, your hell
did I enquire properly into?

For years then I forgot you, I put you down,
ingratitude is the necessary curse
of making things new:
I brought my family to see me through,
I brought my homage & my soft remorse,
I brought a book or two

only, including in the end your last
strange poems made under the shadow of death
Your high figures float
again across my mind and all your past
fills my walled garden with your honey breath
wherein I move, a mote.

The Irish sunshine is lovely but a Belfast man
last night made a pass at my wife: Henry, who had passed out,
was horrified
to hear this news when he woke. The Irish sunshine
is lovely as it comes & goes. The country is full of con-men
as well as the lovely good.

Saints throng these shores, & ancient practices
continue in the dolmens, ruined castles
are standard.
The whole place is ghostly: no wonder Yeats believed in fairies
& personal survival. A trim suburban villa
also is haunted, by me.

Heaven made this place, also, assisted by men,
great men & weird. I see their shades move past
in full daylight.
The holy saints make the trees' tops shiver,
in the all-enclosing wind. And will love last
further than tonight?

Penniless, ill, abroad, Henry lay skew
to Henry's American fate, which was to be well,
have money in the bank
& be at home. He can't think what to do
under this cluster of misfortune & hell,
he gave a last wave & sank

back on his rented pillow, sore at heart,
amazed. It's time for cables to come to the rescue
but cables do not come.
He could have done with just a certain sum
of what was due him: plus the pain, there's smart
& puzzlement too.

Pity his vigil, far away, done for
almost, & choiceless. The fickle Irish sky
shines down for a change,
stopping short of his pillow. His thought tore.
Were there any other gods he could defy,
he wondered, or re-arrange?

Behind me twice her necessary knight
she comes like one of Spenser's ladies on
on a white palfrey
and it is cold & full dark in the valley,
though I haven't seen a dragon for days, & faint moonlight
gives my horse footing till dawn.

My lady is all in green, for innocence
I am in black, a terror to my foes
who are numerous & strong.
I haven't lost a battle yet but I am tense
for the first losing. I wipe blood from my nose
and raise up my voice in song.

Hard lies the road behind, hard that ahead
but we are armed & armoured & we trust
entirely one another.
We have beaten down the foulest of them, lust,
and we pace on in peace, like sister & brother,
doing that to which we were bred.

Blow upon blow, his fire-breath hurt me sore,
I upped my broad sword & it hurt him more,
without his talons at a loss
& dragons are stupid: I wheeled around to the back of him
my charger swift and then I trimmed him
tail-less.

Offering dragons quarter is no good,
they re-grow all their parts & come on again,
they have to be killed.
I set my lance & took him as I would,
in the fiery head, he crumpled like a man,
and one prophecy was fulfilled:

that thrice for Lady Valerie I would suffer
but not be wax from like a base-born duffer,
no no, Sir Henry would win.
until a day that was not prophesied,
having restored her lands. My love & pride
fixed me like a safety-pin.

My mother threw a tantrum on a high terrace
hurling down water-bombs on my brother & me,
none of which landed?
after a panic scene in a restaurant
& in the street: I had picked out for her a peach sweet
instead of one with a Catholic name.

Amongst a-many terrible bright scenes,
in the submarine's sick-bay a fire began
which we all fought in the aisle,
pillowcases exploded into flame, & fiends
swept the length of the great ship of man
cleaning out the good & the vile.

Henry with joy lay down for his next bout of rest,
in happy expectation of the next
assault on his divided soul.
Does the validity of the dream-life suppose a Maker?
If so what a careless monster he must be, whole,
taking the claws with the purr.

Happy & idle, songless Henry swung
next spring, seeing his methodical toils fordone:
congratulate him.
Ha ha, money, money, money, rung
by rung, swaying in the seastorm, without sun,
eyeless in the spray & grim

he counts the anxious months to his arriving:
toils without surcease: wicked nights: ill dreams
wherein Valerie not to his side
(considering all the conditions) streams
and *all* his friends deserted from his striving
save two, skilled & wide

& wise: for them alone he sacked his brain
& for Miss Carver, who was ruth itself
& who will visit here
come spring: my wife will make her right as rain
and Henry's work, on the Atlantic Shelf
will begin to disappear.

Having escaped, except in his dreams, many dooms
and it does not seem likely now that his old phantasy,
of having his left leg sawed off
at the knee, without anesthetic, will come off—
he can see & hear, convalescent Henry:
his house has many rooms

whereof from one he'll cable his doctor if
they are about, after a final game of pingpong,
to take off his left leg
& flame the stump—that goes with the story—
& bandage it, & shriek a cripple Song,
& buy himself a peg:

peg-leg, peg-leg, his golden voice did aria
the better for his change, he could play pingpong
sitting down
& *there* was one leg no more could happen to—
I thrust a knife into it, it doesn't hurt,
as they took it away downtown.

Steps almost unfamiliar toward his door
deep in night came. 'I am a fierce old man'
Henry called out.
Was it his mother? Might it be a whore
out of his youth? Some foe—cold his blood ran—
forgotten in the crowd

female he'd known through hairy years come back
from Themiscyra come to Pussy-cat land
in helmets & miniskirts—
see them all down the Mall! But this attack
was singular: he waited: a soft hiss
bad to his ears, & hurts,

borne through the open transom to his wincing bed:
it was not her, nor her, nor her: was then it *She*
cold in steel & sworded
& unforgiving: Pentheselia dread!
His nerves hear the lock turn. 'I am—' cried Henry,
waking sweated & sordid.

O land of Connolly & Pearse, what have
ever you done to deserve these tragic masters?
You come & go,
free: nothing happens. Nelson's Pillar blows
but the busses still go there: nothing is changed,
for all these disasters O

We fought our freedom out a long while ago
I can't see that it matters, we can't help you
land of ruined abbeys,
discredited Saints & brainless senators,
roofless castles, enemies of Joyce & Swift,
enemies of Synge,

enemies of Yeats & O'Casey, hold your foul ground
your filthy cousins will come around to you,
barely able to read,
friends of Patrick Kavanagh's & Austin Clarke's
those masters who can both read & write,
in the high Irish style.

I gave my love a cookie, as I said,
which she ate. 'Apu-Apu' was my dream.
My love was all in green,
as I said. 'Unam Sanctam' was my other dream,
in a chapel where none of my family could take degrees,
only start them, & mother was dead

I knelt at a shallow altar high on the right
where she had prayed. The carpet was blue-green.
The scholarly frame was French,
Goguel & Guignebert & the Ecole des Hautes Etudes:
I took my mother's hand, which would never hold a degree,
and shook it, behind her back.

I gave my love a cookie, it was her fate
to be involved with Henry Pussycat,
I feel only pity for her.
I'll spare her all I can, in Ireland & elsewhere,
It must have been that cookie which she ate,
never take cookies from cats.

Churchill was ever-active & crammed with glee,
Henry was morbid, inactive, & a child to Angst,
there the difference ends.
They both drank, heavily.
But that is not the reason why this witty
& sportive dinosaur is a hero to Henry & amongst

Henry's friends, given a different turn of luck,
would valiantly have figured. Both wrote things down,
both thought on their feet,
and both spent the bulk of their long lives out of favour:
no bed of roses cushioned any frown
disabling their achievement:

Malice was their appointed air, & with defeat
they were fully familiar: in the end the grand triumph
came down like lightning on one
matchless, & now that's over     let's see what will happen to
    the second
still in full tide, with a style stern wicked & sweet
and O much, so much to be done.

# *An Elegy for W.C.W., the lovely man*

Henry in Ireland to Bill underground:
Rest well, who worked so hard, who made a good sound
constantly, for so many years:
your high-jinks delighted the continents & our ears:
you had so many girls your life was a triumph
and you loved your one wife.

At dawn you rose & wrote—the books poured forth—
you delivered infinite babies, in one great birth—
and your generosity
to juniors made you deeply loved, deeply:
if envy was a Henry trademark, he would envy you,
especially the being through.

Too many journeys lie for him ahead,
too many galleys & page-proofs to be read,
he would like to lie down
in your sweet silence, to whom was not denied
the mysterious late excellence which is the crown
of our trials & our last bride.

Control it now, it can't do any good,
your grief for your great friend, killed on the day
he &     his wife &     three
were moving to a larger house across the street.
Our dead frisk us, & later they get better at it,
our wits are stung astray

till all that we can do is groan, bereft:
tears fail: and then we reckon what is left,
not what was lost.
I notice at this point a divided soul,
headed both fore & aft and guess which soul
will swamp & lose:

that hoping forward, brisk & vivid one
of which will nothing ever be heard again.
Advance into the past!
Henry made lists of his surviving friends
& of the vanished on their uncanny errands
and took a deep breath.

My right foot being colder than my left knee,
I put it on it: my right arm is under the pillow
which is vertical,
transverse never: my right cheek's happy on it, stale
sweat developing over hours makes me changey,
I shift straight over on my back, see,

& my thoughts are different & more straightforward
than on my side, much less my seldom stomach:
half-dreams cease:
O yes, if Henry wants a little peace
in the vigils long he rights onto his back,
he can't sleep but the horde

of terrors fresh from Henry's shaming past
can't get him either, on his back. Years fly
& yet this programme is sound:
fast on your side lie, pal, with one knee fast
under your chin, the horrid waking night, why,
it beats underground
                    (or I reserve my opinion).

Freud was some wrong about dreams, or almost all;
besides his insights grand, he thought that dreams were a transcript
of childhood & the day before,
censored of course: *a* transcript:
even his lesser insight were misunderstood & became a bore
except for the knowing & troubled by the Fall.

Grand Jewish ruler, custodian of the past,
our paedegogue to whip us into truth,
I sees your long story,
tyrannical & triumphant all-wise at last
you wholly failed to take into account youth
& had no interest in your glory.

I tell you, Sir, you have enlightened but
you have misled us: a dream is a panorama
of the whole mental life,
I took one once to forty-three structures, that
accounted in each for each word: I did not yell 'mama'
nor did I take it out on my wife.

—I write with my stomach: Henry ruefully;
and my stomach is improved, I write with my purse
and long sums have come
from foreign places. I write here by the sea
& the gulls go over my gardens. I write terse
& the wastebaskets fill like home.

I write what I design, groaned mortal Henry.
Happiness was ours too but did not stay,
neither misery may.
The moneys & the tummy grew to a gale
wafting him onward where he would not ail
but invent endlessly.

'I helped to wind the clock' cried The O'Rahilly,
'I come to hear it strike'—so in at the death
Henry required to be.
He brought his ancient brain, his faultless breath,
his liver & his lights, his grand energy,
& flourisht like a sycamore tree.

Henry on LSD was Henry indeed
pounds shillings pence, made a mountaining landscape
His foes were Parker green
All his relatives danced in shameless air
Coke came from his nose    The Vatican was a grape
the baby's animals tear

Blue flew the parents through the humid dusk,
they can't arrange for the yellow collection of shells
whimper near the city centre
He told a dirty story, angry & brusque,
He ate black-eyed peas since there was nothing else
He looked everywhere for his mentor

His mentor found was black & ripe, a floater,
we'll thread the eyes, argued the oldest one,
& bury it at sea
To get rid of the shroud put on Full the motor,
just a little hump, sink it in the rising sun,
abominable & impenetrable Henry.

The Twiss is a tidy bundle, chirped joyous Henry,
all other dreams forgotten. Acres of joy
spring when she strode the bike
behind her mother, all so near the sea
where never she has been. A little boy
is what is Daddy's mike,

that which he seeks & fears ha ha. He's *supposed* to fear,
since everyone else does, but actually he can't make it.
He broadcasts freely.
Cantons of candy for the Little Twiss here.
She won a prize on board, one at the church,
at the supermarket

& in the hotel she was extravagantly admired,
I wonder it doesn't turn her silly head,
the little baby.
Universal clouds, an Irish sky,
said what would be her fate, tears & a child
and a father old & wild.

This is the third. What have I more to say
except that I hope that in my dying hour
nobody will be ashamed of me:
May I not be scared then of that final void
into which I lapse, leaving all my power
& memory behind me.

There's a lot of hair in Ireland, much of it red.
An ultimate segment of Irishmen are dead.
Climb over the tombs
to find the gay living at your feet, the intellectual girl
with good legs & fingers at her brow, listening to a whirl
of talk from her companions:

Yeats listened once, he found it did him good,
he died in full stride, a good way to go,
making them wonder what's missing,
a strangeness in the final notes, never to be resolved,
Beethoven's, Goya's: you had better go to the Prado
downstairs, to see on what I am insisting.

Trunks & impedimenta. My manuscript won't go
in my huge Spanish briefcase, some into a bag.
Packing is an India's women's,
I wonder every time how I manage it
& I have done it thirty-four times, by count.
It's time to settle down-O

but not yet. I want to hear the interminable sea
and my spiritual exercises for other civilizations
are well under weigh.
Ships I love, & on ships strangers: Yvette Choinais,
the little man from Cambridge with the little beard
padding about alone barefoot with a little book.

Him Henry never met, but Mlle Choinais
he self-met & swung with on the penultimate day:
O there was a fearful loss,
we could have talked the whole week's journey through
parmi some chaste chat about me & you
and of not being married at twenty-seven the semi-cross

And now I've sent, custodian of Songs,
many to some: which will surprise them,
though they'd all askt.
As for the rest, Henry sounds like eighty Viet Congs
in their little sweet ears: no stratagem
with which he has been tasked

will ever bring those babies into camp,
hurrah: will never bring. Henry's listeners
make up a gallant few,
as I have said before: bring nearer the lamp,
we'll find them out, with lightning, in the torrents
that are merely Henry's due

and are good to the land: merciful rain
beats back & forth, completing the destruction of his roses.
He woke & rose again
to circumambulate the least of houses
where he found no damage, save to the flowers
which were only by rental ours.

Thrums up from nowhere a distinguisht wail,
the griefs of all his grievous friends, and his,
startling Ballsbridge,
our sedate suburb, the capital of What Is,
a late September fly     goes by, learned & frail,
and Cemetery Ridge

glares down the years of losses to this end
that the note from my bank this morning was stampt with
   Sir Roger Casement,
no 'Sir,' just the portrait & years:
about whom Yeats was so wrong
This distinguisht & sensitive man lived in the grip
of a homosexual obsession, even the 'tools' of native policemen
excited him.

Yeats knew nothing about life: it was all symbols
& Wordsworthian egotism: Yeats on Cemetery Ridge
would not have been scared, like you & me,
he would have been, before     the bullet that was his,
studying the movements of the birds,
said disappointed & amazed Henry.

In his complex investigations of death
he called for a locksmith, to burst the topic open
where so many friends have gone
It's crowded there, or lonely, I can't say which,
no messages return, they preserve silence
including the great author of *The Leopard*.

Whom Henry never met: he would have liked to do
& they could have talked about Shakespeare & Stendhal
for sunny weeks
After a great while Henry would murmur: I honour you
(with emphasis his life have seldom demanded, pal):
great men can spring on us in a second:

our heads must be held ready for a nod,
encountering a mystery: I nod to Rolfe
& all the other unpopulars
including that worst career, whose was it? God's
I seem to remember, he makes me wish I had taken up golf
or the study of the stars.

Henry as a landlord made his eight friends laugh
but Henry laughed not: the little scraggly-bearded jerk
has not paid his rent for two months:
a commercial xxxx, with two children:
if they couldn't afford the house, why move into it?
Grrrrrr.

This passion bothered his importunate thought
three thousand miles away & made him wild
with complicated rage:
at the jerk, at himself for a fool, at all mathematicians
except Weyl & Einstein who walked off with his umbrella
leaving his even shabbier own.

I say I'll have the law on scraggly-beard
and he will pay both through his nose & ass,
I'll blacklist him.
But what a bore it is, being a landlord:
so help me Christ, it's worse than a hasty Mass
or a tuneless hymn.

The mind is incalculable. Greatly excited
to learn from his ex-fiancée, a widow,
that she had remarried
I patted the husband on the shoulder and
abruptly my happy thought became financial:
my god, said Henry to himself,

as they shook hands, that suit cost two hundred dollars!
That lucky fellow, with such a bride & such a down-soft tweed!
Vile envy did not enter his soul
but whisked around the corners all-right. Wow.
Henry missed his chance: he sat down to read
& write, missing the whole

girl or lady & the remarkable tweed.
Shall he put in play again the broad esteem
in which his work was held
agonized? his lonely & his desperate work?
O yes: he would not trade: moments of supreme joy jerk
him on, his other loves quelled & dispelled.

According to the Annals of the Four Masters
the West Doorway of the Nuns' Church, Clonmacnoise,
was completed in 1167.
Henry was at that strange point still in Heaven
and so were all his readers. Adrienne & William
slept in possibility,

their wits unwakened, and so did Delmore & Randall
& every reader else upon the earth
or under it.
In a happy proto-silence they or we all waited.
In fact it may be said our breath was bated
waiting for the adventure of sin.

Which took us some one way & some another
like a British traveller in the airport at Bangkok
sweatless among the Orient
reading precisely a dark-blue World's Classics—
I'll bet he loved his father & his mother
which was almost more than Henry could make.

# 339

A maze of drink said: I    will help you through the world.
It is not worse than Hobbes said, nor as bad.
Though he was a thoughtful man.
Aubrey has done him for us forever. The flag unfurled
by the American Embassy each morning lifts my heart,
Henry was a shameless patriot.

At the flagstaff head the fine flag cracked like a whip
slatting the halyards. Diplomatic brains
I suppose unfurl
each morning, so difficult are our relations with Ireland,
the other Massachusetts. Strong winds are tossing Irish trees
& putting my heart in a whirl.

The greenhouse door was left open. Seagulls were screeching.
Across his face came a delicious breeze.
The gale was through.
Cats-paws of wind still ruffled the black water.
One gold line along the rubbingstrake
signalled a beauty.

The secret is not praise. It's just being accepted
at something like the figure where you put your worth
anywhere on the bloody earth,
especially abroad. We must keep our spirits up
*anyhow*. Of course, praise is nice too,
particularly when it comes to a stop.

When it comes to a stop, so one can think 'Yes, that happened.'
It's not so good while going on: an element of incredulity
enters & dominates.
The shadows of the grey ash on my page,
I can't get out of this either to youth or age,
I'm stuck with middle.

*Such* hard work demands such international thanks
besides better relations with one's various banks,
slightly better.
So many have forgotten me, I forget some
and there will never come a congregation
to see needing Henry home.

## The Dialogue, aet. 51

Imperishable Henry glared at the map
of the monastic remains in Ireland & felt threatened.
(His wife gave it him: 7/6).
He felt declared, well, out of bounds, say; crap.
The soul's unreal! will you have your death unsweetened
or must I trot out again these stones & sticks

to be companion in 'your' pilgrimage?
Perishable Henry groaned, familiar too well
with the routines of decay.
His body kn w it had to suffer, and rage
contorted its anti-Buddhist features. Still,
the body is I ving its day.

The body is having its day, & so is Henry:
winning tributes, given prizes, made offers, & such.
Only the terrible soul
had no inkling of what was to come for he,
he stood by his instinct & it was not much—
I hear the Devil likes them whole.

Fan-mail from foreign countries, is that fame?
Imitations & parodies in your own,
translations?
Most of the relevant prizes, your private name
splashed on page one, with a photograph alone
or you with your lovely wife?

Interviews on television & radio
on various continents, can that be fame?
Henry could not find out.
Before he left the ship at Cobh he was photographed,
I don't know how they knew he was coming
He said as little as possible.

They wanted to know whether        his sources of inspiration
might now be Irish: I cried out 'of course'
& waved him off with my fountain pen.
The tender left the liner & headed for shore.
Cobh (pronounced Khōve) approached, our luggage was ready,
and anonymously we went into Customs.

A lone letter from a young man: that is fame.

Another directory form to be corrected.
Henry did one years & years agone for *Who's Who*,
wasn't that enough?
Why does the rehearsal of the public events of his life
always strike him as a list of failures, pal?
Where is childhood,

from which he recovered, & where are the moments of love?
his three-day drunk at the fête of St Tropez?
his inn-garden in Kyoto?
his moments with Sonya? the pool-apron in Utah whereon he lay
the famous daughter? of the famous mother? O
there were more than enough whereof

to whet an entry, rather than this silliness
of jobs, awards, books. He took a hard look
at the programme of the years
and struck his hardened palms across his ears
& 'Basta!' cried: I should     have been a noted crook
or cat in a loud slum yes.

# Herbert Park, Dublin

Were you góod tó him? He was not to you:
I know: it was in his later years
when he could not be good to anybody:
pain & disorder, baseless fears,
malign influences
ruled his descending star,

which crowds today my thought from observation
of this most beautiful of parks since Bombay
on this éxquisite October Sunday,
the great bright green spaces under the fine sun,
children & ducks & dogs, two superb elms,
the scene Henry overwhelms.

We traverse a trellis, magisterial.
A little is rolling over & over      on the turf, my own.
That dreadful small-hours hotel death mars all.
Did you leave him all alone,
to that end? or did he leave you, to seek
frailty & tremor, obsessed, mad & weak?

Anarchic Henry thought of laying hands
on Henry: haw! but the blood & the disgrace,
no, no, that's out.
They cut off, in Attic law, that hand from the body
and burying it elsewhere. That I understands,
but the destruction of the face

quickly is what leaves this avenue unused
and I have never discussed with anyone amused
this,
which has filled out many conversaziones
on several continents: relevant experts
say the wounds to the survivors is

the worst of the Act, the worst of the Act! Sit still,
maybe the goblins will go away, leaving you free,
your breath coming normally,
all quarrels made up, say it took twenty letters
some to his inferiors, two to his betters
so-called, pal.

Henry's *very* rich American friends
drifted through Henry's lean establishment
on the way to salmon-fishing 60 miles north,
on the Fane, & the Irish theatre
and all these friends were almost equally interesting,
the wives even more so than the vivid husbands.

A 13-pounder, two feet long, taking up his whole back,
gaffed we saw, and a very pretty fish.
We caught nothing.
It is in the nature of Henry to catch nothing,
but not of Ed's: crept into his phantastic optimism
a definite note of lack.

But that good man, stranded with all his dough,
uncertain, having travelled many paths,
of his vocation, FREE,
seemed once or twice to be wanting guidance O
which nobody can give: he is *too* free,
he needs the limitations of Henry.

The day was dark. The day was hardly day.
Forgestic Henry, with no more to say,
gloomed at his big front window,
& saucy lawn with gentians hard to see
and brooded on his almost endless destiny
with a birthday to come O.

Hankered he less for youth than for more time
to adjust the conflicting evidence, the 'I'm—
immortal-&-not' routine,
Pascal, Spinoza, & Augústine,
Kafka & all his tribe, living it out alone,
Mary Baker Eddy's telephone

in her vault with a direct line to the *Monitor:*
it ain't rung yet, pal, nor has Christ returned,
according to the *World Almanac*
which I read less for what it say than for
what's missing: the editor of the *Atlantic* burned,
for instance, & Christ came back.

700 years? It's too soon to decide,
an anti-instant of God's anti-time: Dante & Rimbaud
with all *their* problems.
But each dug down for himself a definite hole
in a definite universe which he could bring to mind
structured, unlike the oblongs

Henry & his surviving friends now truly confront
when a whore can almost overthrow a government
on front pages all over the world
& be a big star afterward: not a woman:
a woman's brow might in that spot be pearled,
her pimp killed himself

she pursued her career, whore Keeler: married & had a child.
Perhaps we ought to forgive her? Reformed perhaps?
Can anyone reach that stupidity of sin?
Complacent, laughing, as      in America we have Lana Turner
whose daughter killed her mother's gangster lover, to
an access of box-office.

The great Bosch in the Prado, castles in Spain,
zen gardens in Kyoto, a tarn in Utah,
pads all over Manhattan,
Henry observed, & the salmon-fishing on the Fane
nearly at the bitter border between the North & South,
& dinner at LaPérouse au gratin,

Henry entranced watched, & the Berkeley Hills
& years of Harvard Yard: Henry got around.
I can't say it improved him
but unquestionably it gave him some to think about:
the temple complex at Bhuwaneshwar,
phantasies where nobody reproved him!

He rested on his laurels after a ski-lift
that showed him four or seven states: he hoped to die
on the down into the void,
his seat so small it had no toilet paper,
while the mountains smiled, at Henry in mid air
& at his equally terrified wife, monfs pregnant.

All the girls, with their vivacious littles,
visited him in dream: he was interested in their tops & bottoms
& even in their middles,
for years Henry had been getting away with *murder*,
the Sheriff mused. There'll have to be an order
specifically to stop climbing trees,

& other people's wives: we'll cut off his telephone,
stroke one, and hasten his senility,
stroke two: encourage his virtues, if he has one:
ask him upstairs more frequently for tea,
stroke four, put him on the wagon, Death,
no drinks: that ought to cure him.

The progress of age helped him, to be not good but better:
he restricted his passes to passes made by letters
he drank less.
Mlle Choinais noted a definite though small improvement in Henry:
as they passed forth across the northern sea,
a degree of gentleness.

Animal Henry sat reading the *Times Literary Supplement*
with a large Jameson & a worse hangover.
Who will his demon lover
today become, he queried. Having made a dent
in the world, he insisted on special treatment,
massage at all hours.

Love in the shadows where the animals *come*
tickled his nerves' ends. He put down *The Times*
& began a salvage operation,
killing that is the partly incoherent,
saving the mostly fine, polishing the surfaces.
Brain- & instinct-work.

On all fours he danced about his cage, poor Henry
for whom, my love, too much was never enough.
Massage me in Kyoto's air.
The Japanese women are better than the Swedes,
more rhythmical, more piercing.
       Somewhere, everywhere
a girl is taking her clothes off.

The Cabin, Congdon St, & the Old Gristmill
saw stretches of the long & long work done
to certain satisfactions,
including Henry's reluctant still & still
from the notion of the work's being a large one
in spite of the incessant additions.

During those years he met his seminars,
went & lectured & read, talked with human beings,
paid insurance & taxes;
but his mind was not on it. His mind was elsewheres
in an area where the soul not talks but sings
& where foes are attacked with axes.

Enemies his pilgrimage duly brought
to bring him down, and they almost succeeded.
He sang on like a harmful bird.
His foes are like footnotes, he figured, sought
chiefly by doctoral candidates: props, & needed,—
comic relief, —absurd.

These massacres of the superior peoples,
the Armenians, the Jews, the Ibos, all
(cried apoplectic Henry)
serve to remind us that culture was only a phase
through which we threaded, coming out at the other end
to the true light again of savagery.

—You feelin bad, Mr Bones? You don't *look* good.
—Do I looking like a man spent years in Hell?
for that is Henry's case:
and he remembers what he saw, how he felt & smelt,
sharp terror that increases & that stays:
the sufferings of wood

when burned are to our sufferings on the earth
as those are to our sufferings hereafter,
that is, for the Evil:
the otherwise will escape & sleep forever
except for those who in their time gave birth
to the consorts of the Devil

The only happy people in the world
are those who do not have     to write long poems:
muck, administration, toil:
the protototality of an absence of contact
in one's own generation, chiefly the old & the young
persisting with interest.

'The Care & Feeding of Long Poems' was Henry's title
for his next essay, which will come out when
he wants it to.
A Kennedy-sponsored bill for the protection
of poets from long poems     will benefit the culture
and do no harm to that kind Lady, Mrs Johnson.

He would have gone to the White House & consulted the President
during his 10 seconds in the receiving line
on the problems of long poems
Mr Johnson has never written one
but he seems a generous & able man
'Tetelestai' said St John.

# Slattery's, in Ballsbridge

Cling to me & I promise you'll drown too,
this voyage is terminal, I'll take your beauty down
and ruined in sea weed
then it will seem forever. I am you
you are your moan, you are your sexy moan,
we are a 'possum treed.

Difficult at midnight grew our love
as if we could not have enough, enough,
reluctant lady.
Nobody in the world knows where I am.
Your hair drags. You would have made a terrific victim
in one of Henry's thrillers.

Weep for the fate of man, excellent lady.
He comes no near, whereas he is so lost,
a crisis in the ghost
baffles endeavour, so he would lie down.
Attend his sorry perish, excellent lady.
Withhold from him your frown.

With fried excitement he looked across at life
wondering if he could bear it more,
wondering,
in the middle of a short war with his wife,
deep in the middle, in short, of a war,
he couldn't say whether to sing

further or seal his lonely     throat, give himself up.
Tomorrow is his birthday, makes you think.
The London *TLS*
are mounting só much of him he could scream.
There was a time he marched from dream to dream
but he seems to be out of ink,

he seems to be out of everything again
save whiskey & cigarettes, both bad for him.
He clapped both hands to both ears
and resigned from the ranks of giving men.
In a minute now he'll wake, distinct & grim.
I'm not, he cried, what I appears.

Henry's pride in his house was almost fierce,
Henry, who took no pride in anything
only but work hard done:
an angry ghost appeared & leaned for years
on his front stoop; elderly Henry spread his wings
one by one by one

until the traffic could not see it more:
he's leaving for America & things,
things.
Deep in concussion, deep in extra love,
he sorted out his extra fate. He sings
& clowns

and is wiser than the next man, in so many towns
across a continent. We must be careful of it,
the special gift,
the wardrobes wide & wider. Pained eyes, Henry's.
Unmanly slovenly love took him at times
and passed him back.

## The Gripe

The price he pays for sleep. Pockets of grief,
wrecked ladies, back in his own country, write
him ruined letters.
He advises in the dark, of woes, near the chief:
her stepfather knew her when she was ten,
since when, her soul is a sight.

With a shudder a troubled girl brought an indictment.
Can so much pain inhabit a simple body
& high-piled, most blonde hair?
A single moan emerged & filled the years.
An inability to respond, in the cheekbones,
the old woman thought.

Moments of horror in deep sleep survived.
Life as a tangle & a hopeless one,
she murmured when she woke.
Her skin showed no disaster but she could not love.
The lady already dead the love of the done
passed on to Henry & broke.

In sleep, of a heart attack, let Henry go.
The end of tennis. The beginning of the dark.
The beginning of the wagon.
It is the onward coming terrifies.
Now at last the effort to make him kill himself
has failed.

Take down the thing then to which he was nailed.
I am a boat was moored on the wrong shelf.
Love has wings & flies.
Amazed it could engineer such agony,
Henry tried the world again     & again, falling short of the mark.
Unblock! let all griefs flow.

There are more over there than over here,
for welcome eerie. The whole city turned out
to rustle Henry home.
He'd made his peace & would no further roam.
He wondered only what it was about.
He felt the news was near.

The universe has gifted me with friends,
was special of it, whom I not deserve
save for my own love back
imperfectly manifested with amends
which Henry had need of, graded on a curve
by certain, Henry on the track

strapped, awaited the train. Instead came a cable
from the most beautiful woman in the United States,
devout & lovely: 'Why do you honor me?'
she weirdly askt. Henry relaxed & stable
but busy busy made reply: 'We awaits
a lady even more worthy of honor:

until then suffer us to make do with you,
which is forever? Gulls here beside the sea
approve poor Henry's choice.
Allow then in our end that we make do
with the mysteries of you which are one mystery'
half-enhanced by Henry's voice.

# 361

## *The Armada Song*

They came ashore with erections
& laid the Irish maidens in large numbers
then in 1588.
Spaniards are vile & virile.
History after all is a matter of fumbles.
Man's derelictions, man's fate,

is a matter of sorry record. Somehow the prizes
come at the wrong times to the proper people
& vice versa.
The great ships, confused in tempest,
drove on the shoals. Accepting ladies
crowded the northern shore.

In they plunged, in half-armour, with their strength
returned to the personal. Philip's on his own.
These fragrant maidens
are good to a man out of the sea, at length,
in a new world, and each new man, alone,
made up his own destiny.

And now I meet you in the thinky place,
you & I, your good brain & hot heart
counselled Henry on
in his heavy labour, O you were good to him
and he was glad to look you in the face
at Yale & Harvard

We have read the same fine writers all our lives
& hoisted the same grave problems: that gives us
somewhat in common, my dear:
allow me to bless your gift, for you are young
and Henry is old, old as a hieroglyph:
we have in common Song:

I raise my voice in your presence in your praise
and if we had been married to each other
I would have made a pass at you,
in Cambridge or New Haven: but as it is
I bless your gift & am grateful for your beauty
& high kindness to Henry.

I cast as feminine Miss Shirley Jones
as she was in *Oklahoma!* and for male
George C. Scott
as he was in *The Hustler:* off stage moans,
we begin with them in bed: if this relation should fail,
if it should not prove hòt,

God bless our fate in the West & do me down
a potent Communist—as we all know,
the peoples in the East
have no sexual problems, have no problems
but housing & food & ideology:
all lesser problems ceased

when criminal attractive Lenin, bald,
went over the frontier in a sealed train
to take over the Revolution.
We know the issue of that, it has been told.
But the issue of Miss Jones & Mr Scott
comes at us, lovely & sane.

*There* is one book that Henry hasn't read:
*Ubu Roi*. He feeling ignorant    whenever his mind brings it up.
Everytime anybody says
—Mr Bones, you has read everything—he singles out instead
*Ubu Roi*, to prove he is an idiot
and should be, as one, blest.

O Henry in his youth read many things:
he gutted the Columbia & the Cambridge libraries
& Widener & Princeton
& the British Museum & the Library of Congress
but mostly he bought books to have as his own
cunningly, like extra wings:

he resorted to the Morgan for Keats' letters
so obscure, so important, one stroke of a pen
deciding his opinion of Milton,
his editors wrong. Henry corrected his betters
as well as his lessers & would have had to say
much but for his different profession.

Back to the Folger!

Henry, a foreigner, lustful & old,
bearded, exasperated, lay in bed
cursing his enemies.
He loved his friends with a thick love, them to hold
to him in all his bad times, which were rife.
Henry living & dead

was full of friends & foes: he had no team-spirit.
He lashed the lapses of those who were to inherit.
He sank back exhausted.
Grimy dreams wore him out. He woke half-sane
& screamed for stronger drinks. Open the main!
Pour, if necessary, drinks down him.

I, Henry Pussy-cat, being in ill-health
& 900 years old, begin & cease,
to doubt.
When my old friend complained to my older friend
'Why don't you come see me more often?'
'I'm afraid you'll find me out.'

# 366

Chilled in this Irish pub I wish my loves
well, well to strangers, well to all his friends,
seven or so in number,
I forgive my enemies, especially two,
races his heart, at so much magnanimity,
can it at all be true?

—Mr Bones, you on a trip outside yourself.
Has you seen a medicine man? You sound will-like,
a testament & such.
Is you going? —Oh, I suffer from a strike
& a strike & three balls: I stand up for much,
Wordsworth & that sort of thing.

The pitcher dreamed. He threw a hazy curve,
I took it in my stride & out I struck,
lonesome Henry.
These Songs are not meant to be understood, you understand.
They are only meant to terrify & comfort.
Lilac was found in his hand.

# Henry's Crisis

In sight of a more peaceful country, just beyond,
& just in sight—ilex & magnolia, land
rimmed by a bountiful sea—
Henry took stock of where he now might be
in his own warring state. He stood perplexed
as to where to go next,

forward or backward: he could not stay still,
the decision came: his rotors floated well
to take him back or ahead.
Here he paused, though, & thought of those whom he was leaving
& those whom he would be missing without grieving
in the fair of the land ahead.

'My friends are full' he muttered to himself,
'I'll make no more, so many now are dead.
*Backward* is the gallant word,
and grapple to my heart the splendid rest,
to leave the new land unknown & undistressed'—
The happy rotors whirred.

At a gallop through his gates came monsters, buoyant
& credible & wild—his people fled
anguisht before them.
Soon the great city was all monsters, high-bred
& parti-coloured, comfy, digging in
like a really bad dream.

New rules were promulgated at the City Centre.
Those with more eyes, cast ruthlessly aside,
lurked to the suburbs.
The airport was closed down. Animals were untied.
Thought of his kind ground & lurched to a halt,
all nouns became verbs.

Was all this the result of a failure of love,
he hailed a passing stranger, a young girl
with several legs.
He heard her shout, remote, 'You is a swirl
of ending dust, Your Majesty . . .' Since when,
he's hunkered down & begs.

I threw myself out helter-skelter-whiz
as goalie to head off a lucky puck.
Henry was tough on that day.
Tricky Dick the coach was pleased, for a change.
He returned the first offense, like a mountain range.
We still lost to The Gunnery, hooray.

At the tea afterward I askt him why
he hadn't replaced mé: he said we were lost,
let the discredit go where it belongs.
Thank you, I call back down the whiskey years—
he came to hear me in     Chicago with both ears—
god knows what he thought of them Songs.

I have more respect for him than I have for me,
and yet I said I headed for respect,
I pickt the wrong field.
Applause was numerous but my orders were sealed:
at forty nearly when I took them out
I gave a joyless shout.

Henry saw with Tolstoyan clarity
his muffled purpose. He described the folds—
not a symbol in the place.
Naked the man came forth in his mask, to be.
Illnesses from encephalitis to colds
shook his depths & his surface.

When he dressed up & up, his costumes varied
with the southeast wind, but he remained aware.
Awareness was most of what he had.
The terrible chagrin to which he was married—
derelict Henry's siege mentality—
stability, I will stay

in my monastery until my death
& the fate my actions have so hardly earned.
The horizon is all cloud.
Leaves on leaves on leaves of books I've turned
and I know nothing, Henry said aloud,
with his ultimate breath.

# Henry's Guilt

Sluggish, depressed, & with no mail to cheer,
he lies in Ireland's rains bogged down, aware
of definite mental pain.
He hasn't a friend for a thousand miles to the west
and only two in London, he counted & guessed:
ladies he might see again.

He has an interview to give in London
but the ladies have never married, frolicsomes
as long ago they were,
must he impute to him their spinsterhood
& further groan, as for the ones he stood
up & married fair?

Connection with Henry seemed to be an acre in Hell,
he crossed himself with horror. Doubtless a bell
ought to've been hung on Henry
to warn a-many lovely ladies off
before they had too much, which was enough,
and set their calves to flee.

O yes I wish her well. Let her come on
to Henry's regions, with her mortal wound.
In so far as repair
is possible, we'll lie her in the sun
forever, with to protect her a great hound,
so that she lies in peace there.

Until her lover comes: let him be good
quietly to her, and her blocked faith restore
in the mountains & the roar
of the grand sea of tumbling pebbles: could
anyone anywhere ask more?
Her patience is exemplary.

Cold & golden lay the high heroine
in a wilderness of bears. Let one man in.
One is enough.
Fish for the master, who will do you well,
rely not on the stormy citadel—
it's a matter of love.

My eyes with which I see so easily
will become closed. My friendly heart will stop.
I won't sit up.
Nose me, soon you won't like it—ee—
worse than a pesthouse; and my thought all gone
& the vanish of the sun.

The vanish of the moon, which Henry loved
on charming nights when Henry young was moved
by delicate ladies
with ripped-off panties, mouths open to kiss.
They say the coffin closes without a sound
& is lowered underground!

So now his thought's gone, buried his body dead,
what now about the adorable *Little* Twiss
& his fair lady,
will they set up a tumult in his praise
will assistant professors become associates
by working on his works?

Drum Henry out, called some. Others called No,
he did a deed once, damn to chastise him so;
the regiment can bear him.
—He tore the precincts down, cried the vicious first.
Learned & stealthy he attacked & cursed
our whole art of arms, holy, dim.

Worse still, he won praise overseas by this,
affording himself his own rules. Well, we hiss
& close our eyes at his freaks.
—You got enemies, Mr Bones. I 'low
a-many will seek your skin & your parts below.
—I have sat here for weeks

and years. There was a time when I almost poisoned my cook.
Unamuno wrote in the Visitors' Book
'a humble man & a tramp'.
No challenges have come. Only the jackals howl
and Henry is fierce in blackness as an owl
on a field-mouse at the edge of my camp.

## His Helplessness

I know a young lady's high-piled ashen hair
and she is miserable, threatened a thoroughfare
for pants in their desire
fondless: she drinks too dear, & feels put down,
'no one is friendly to me' she scribbles here,
of all them griefs the crown

having been her lay by her father agèd ten
from which she grew up slowly into the world of men
who headed ha for her.
She put her soul in jeopardy with pills
a week ago, she writes—Henry would offer,
only it's thousands of miles,

help to the delicate lady far in her strait,
counsel she needs, needs one to pace her fate.
I cannot spot a hole,
& I look with my heart, in her darkness over there:
dark shroud the clouds on her disordered soul
whose last letter flew like a prayer.

# 376

Christmas again, when you're supposed to be happiest.
The tree's decorated, the baby's agog with joy
& Santa is a white-thatched boy
down our main small chimney with his best.
I hope he makes, we had to have it swept
after one fierce day when flames leapt.

We must live alone; he did; it deepens.
Falling & burning soot is not pleasing:
we thought we'd lose the house.
Pride power loneliness, each in its season,
brought Henry up to three marriages
as up to Penn Station came Christian Gauss

there to drop dead, surround & alone
(Charmed swam the hero of the Hellespont)
as Gaudi on the street in Barcellona.
The fair lose more, having them more to lose
& the good & the geniuses.
Spent dangles of his life in colleges.

Then he limpt down the stairs & left the house

Father Hopkins, teaching elementary Greek
whilst his mind climbed the clouds, also died here.
O faith in all he lost.
Swift wandered mad through his rooms & could not speak.
A milkman sane died, the one one, I fear.
His name was gone almost.

Hopkins's credits, while the Holy Ghost
rooted for Hopkins, hit the Milky Way.
This is a ghost town.
It's Xmas. Henry, can you reach the post?
Yeats did not die here—died in France, they say,
brought back by a warship & put down.

Joyce died overseas also but Hopkins died here:
where did they plant him, after the last exam?
To his own lovely land
did they rush him back, out of this hole unclear,
barbaric & green, or did they growl 'God's damn'
the lousy Jesuit, canned.

The beating of a horse fouled Nietszche's avatar,
thereafter never said he one sane word,
Henry is not like that
but the fear.
They're treading on toes notoriously tender.
The sudden sun sprang out

I gave the woman & her child ten shillings,
I can't bear beggars at my door, and I
cannot bear at my door
the miserable, accusing me, and sore
back to my own country would I go
transparent, through the sky.

From fearful heart into an ice-cold pool,
Texas Falls in Vermont: delicious tremor.
Let's have that again.
No, that will not return. Henry, the Lord of beauty,
is cashing in his problems
The violent winds in my gardens front & back
have driven away my birds

To the edge of Europe, the eighteenth edge,
the ancient edge, Henry sailed full of thought
and rich with high-wrought designs,
for a tranquil mind & to fulfil a pledge
he gave himself to end a labour, sought
but now his mind not finds

conformable itself to that forever
or any more of the stretch of Henry's years.
Strange & new outlines
blur the old project. Soon they dissever
the pen & the heart, the old heart with its fears
& the daughter for which it pines.

Fresh toils the lightning over the Liffey, wild
and the avenues, like Paris's, are rain
and Henry is here for a while
of many months, along with the squalls of a child,
thirty years later. I will not come again
or not come with this style.

# *From the French Hospital*
# *in New York, 901*

Wordsworth, thou form almost divine, cried Henry,
'the egotistical sublime' said Keats,
oh ho, you lovely man!
make from the rafters some mere sign to me
whether when after this raving heart which beats
& which to beat began

Long so years since     stops     I may (ah) expect
a fresh version of living or if I stop
wholly.
Oblongs attend my convalescence, wreckt
and now again, by many full propt up,
not irreversible Henry.

Punctured Henry wondered would he die
forever, all his fine body forever lost
and his very useful mind?
Hopeless & violent the man will lie,
on decades' questing, whose crazed hopes have crossed
to wind up here blind.

Cave-man Henry grumbled to his spouse
'It's cold in here. I'd rather have a house.
A house would be better,'
The bear-robe did them fairly well, but still
they certainly might fall ill.
I'm writing Mr Antelope a letter.

Leslie we lost all down the pure rock-face
& that was terrifying. Junior tried a trip in space
& ever since then he'll stutter.
I woke our wiseman over an awful dream:
vividest his shrew-spouse: Scream.
I'm writing Mr Antelope a letter.

And with great good luck I'll say a little more.
I am frightened by the waves upon the shore,
& seldom steal there, wetter
with the wild rain but safe, & back to the cave.
What he rendered forward too he forgave.
I'm writing Mr Antelope a letter.

At Henry's bier let some thing fall out well:
enter there none who somewhat has to sell,
the music ancient & gradual,
the voices solemn but the grief subdued,
no hairy jokes but everybody's mood
subdued, subdued,

until the Dancer comes, in a short short dress
hair black & long & loose, dark dark glasses,
uptilted face,
pallor & strangeness, the music changes
to 'Give!' & 'Ow!' and how! the music changes,
she kicks a backward limb

on tiptoe, pirouettes, & she is free
to the knocking music, sails, dips, & suddenly
returns to the terrible gay
occasion hopeless & mad, she weaves, it's hell,
she flings to her head a leg, bobs, all is well,
she dances Henry away.

It brightens with power, when the dawn begins.
My court emerges. Up its shutters throws
my kiosk.
So cigarettes are here, and many sins
are purged by a dreamless night. I pick my nose.
All men have made mistakes.

All men have made mistakes: that includes You.
August in Athens, at the end of the labour.
Come kiss me.
I saw your fault before you showed it me,
the tall Anglaise, unmarried, 29.
So erect, so fine.

Grant her a husband, bête Apollo, swiftly.
She was not born for sacrifice, I think.
But she was born.
My baby's all hunched up, in sleep. Poseidon,
ruined on Sounion, cares, in the hard cold wind,
who gave hell to Odysseus.

The marker slants, flowerless, day's almost done,
I stand above my father's grave with rage,
often, often before
I've made this awful pilgrimage to one
who cannot visit me, who tore his page
out: I come back for more,

I spit upon this dreadful banker's grave
who shot his heart out in a Florida dawn
O ho alas alas
When will indifference come, I moan & rave
I'd like to scrabble till I got right down
away down under the grass

and ax the casket open ha to see
just how he's taking it, which he sought so hard
we'll tear apart
the mouldering grave clothes ha & then Henry
will heft the ax once more, his final card,
and fell it on the start.

My daughter's heavier. Light leaves are flying.
Everywhere in enormous numbers turkeys will be dying
and other birds, all their wings.
They never greatly flew. Did they wish to?
I should know. Off away somewhere once I knew
such things.

Or good Ralph Hodgson back then did, or does.
The man is dead whom Eliot praised. My praise
follows and flows too late.
Fall is grievy, brisk. Tears behind the eyes
almost fall. Fall comes to us as a prize
to rouse us toward our fate.

My house is made of wood and it's made well,
unlike us. My house is older than Henry;
that's fairly old.
If there were a middle      ground between things and the soul
or if the sky resembled more the sea,
I wouldn't have to scold

                                        my heavy daughter.

# Index of First Lines

415

417

# Index of Titles

427